Avalanche! Hasty Search

The Care and Training of Avalanche Search and Rescue Dogs

Patti Burnett

Copyright © 2003 by Patti Burnett

All rights reserved. No part of this publication may be reproduced or transmitted in any form or by any means, electronically or mechanically, including photocopying, recording, or by any information storage or retrieval system, without the prior written permission of the publisher.

Published by Doral Publishing, Phoenix, Arizona
Printed in the United States of America.

Edited by Karin Ashe
Interior Design by The Printed Page
Cover Design by 1106 Design

Library of Congress Card Number: 2003100551
ISBN: 0-944875-95-5

Acknowledgments and Contributors

There are insufficient words to thank the many people who contributed to the writing of this book. Sandy Bryson and her beautiful Shepherds inspired me to reach for a higher level in training and trust in the abilities of these incredible creatures. We all have much to continue to learn from her books and her training seminars.

Thank you, Chuck Tolton for believing that the avalanche dog could become a reality, even when it was just a dream in our heads.

Various handlers and their dogs provided stories and their names are mentioned throughout the work. They continue to give so selflessly of their time and energies so that others may live.

Veterinarians, Dr. Paul Veralli and Dr. Tom Fatora were there for every stitch and every joint x-ray. Thank you Tom for believing that we could make the Avalanche Dog Training Video and finding the time that wasn't there for editing and copying. Thank you, Paul, for discovering Sandy's cancer while still at an early stage.

Susan Bulanda, as a published search dog author, encouraged me to move ahead and not get discouraged when I came up against obstacles as a new author. Thank you for believing in me.

Thank you Sandy, McFarland and Timberee Goldens, for your generous donation of the fluff-ball we know as Sandy. He far exceeded all of our expectations. Thank you for writing the section in this book on canine structure.

Jenny Hager, Bob Winsett, and Cullen Lyle provided many of the photographs in this book. Thank you for generously giving of your time and talents to more completely illustrate those concepts that I could not as capably put into words.

Thank you, Charlene Woodward and Dogwise for reviewing early copies of the manuscript and giving me good recommendations.

Thank you, Bethany and Rachel, for allowing your Mom to travel to various places to do research and learn from those more experienced. Forgive me for the birthday that I missed and the school performance that had to take second place to missions and conferences. I know you both wanted to go to Switzerland with us. Next time.

My husband, Dan, has been there throughout the conception of this book. From the purchase of our first SAR puppy, Hasty, to the many hours slaving over the computer, he has provided support and encouragement. Thanks for always being willing to be buried, even before we knew how to build the more luxurious caves.

Mom and Dad, thanks for challenging and believing in me. You deserve credit for instilling in me the wonder and awesomeness of God's creation, and these dogs that He made are a beautiful illustration of who He is.

Finally, thank you, Hasty, for giving your life so that others could live. I never doubted that when I gave you an assignment, you would do it to the best of your ability. You have been an inspiration to Sandy and I and all the other dog teams that have followed your trail. Good dog. Sleep well, my friend, knowing that your task has been completed. Free dog.

Hasty sitting outside Copper Mountain Ski Patrol Headquarters, by Jenny Hager

Foreword

Dear Reader,

Over the years, search and rescue dog handlers have requested resources to assist them in training avalanche dogs. While many excellent books are available on the subject of search and rescue (SAR) dogs, there are none dedicated specifically to the discipline of avalanche. In the mid-90's, Dr. Tom Fatora and I produced the video "Avalanche Dog Training." This book is a labor of love and an attempt to enlarge upon our earlier efforts. It is the product of many years of SAR training and missions.

Above all, I want to help you and your canine partner reach your greatest avalanche hunting potential. It is essential to recognize, from the start, that this is a team effort; and without a total commitment on your part, your endeavors will fail. If you do not have a canine partner yet, you are at an advantage because you have the opportunity to start clean.

I have had the privilege of studying and searching under some of the best avalanche technicians, dog handlers, and dogs in the country, including my four legged partners, Hasty and Sandy. We have worked with the Copper Mountain Ski Patrol, Summit County Rescue Group, and Search and Rescue Dogs of Colorado for more than two decades. Our home of Summit County, Colorado has the dubious distinction of being at the epicenter of avalanche accidents and deaths in the United States. With little warning in our developmental years, my first rescue dog, Hasty, and I were hurled into the thick of avalanche rescue—ready or not. I count it a privilege and profound responsibility to share some of our experiences with you. I caution you to be ready when your time comes to make a difference in the lives of others.

Please do not confuse this text with an avalanche safety manual. People with far more experience and skill have already expounded upon such information. I will reference some of those publications in the appendix of this book. It is your responsibility to read those books and take the necessary courses. I welcome your input as you strive to implement the techniques of Hasty Search.

Thank you for giving me the opportunity to acquaint you with avalanche dogs, especially Hasty, one of my most loyal companions.

Patti Burnett
Supervisor, Dog Trainer, and EMT, Copper Mountain Ski Patrol
Dog Handler and Mission Coordinator, Summit County Rescue Group
Dog Handler, Search and Rescue Dogs of Colorado

Hasty & Patti basking in the joy of a successful avalanche training session, by Dave Buchanon

Contents

Acknowledgements and Contributors iii

Foreword v

Chapter 1. Handler Preparation 1

Chapter 2. Equipment. 13

Chapter 3. Puppy Selection 25

Chapter 4. Training 43

Chapter 5. Avalanche Dog Training Progression. 61

Chapter 6. The Health of Your Avalanche Dog 79

Chapter 7. Scent and Snow 95

Chapter 8. Certification 103

Chapter 9. Search Strategy 111

Chapter10. Mission Base. 125

Chapter11. Public Relations & Avalanche Awareness 137

Chapter12. Missions 143

Chapter13. Goodbye, My Friend 195

Glossary 207

Appendix. 215

Bibliography 225

Resources 226

Index 227

SAR Hasty
April 8, 1986—April 10, 2000

Our friend and companion, Hasty was deployed on his final mission at 1600 on April 10, 2000. Since January, Hasty had endured seven grand mal seizures, which became increasingly debilitating with each event. Dan called me to come home on Monday, because Hasty had had another seizure. When I took him for his last walk, not a wag could be found in his golden tail; he even refused the biscuit I offered him. Life is getting bad for a Golden Retriever when he refuses a biscuit and a walk. Hasty was having no fun.

No working dog had a greater life than Hasty. In his unusually long SAR career, he was operational for nearly 12 years. Hasty was certified in water, avalanche, and wilderness airscent through Search and Rescue Dogs of Colorado and an active member of the Copper Mountain Ski Patrol and Summit County Rescue Group. He responded to nearly 150 missions, with many successful finds. He was the first SAR dog in Summit County and paved the way for other ski areas and search groups to incorporate rescue dogs.

He gave us innumerable memories, but some of my favorite Hasty stories are:

- *At 6 months old, Hasty rode Sierra chairlift at Copper all by himself. He loved to go for a ride, whether it was in a helicopter, airplane, fire engine, snowcat, snowmobile, toboggan, motorboat, canoe, sailboard, motorhome, zodiac, chairlift, or car.*

- *At one year of age, Hasty was swept down an irrigation ditch while training. Before I could haul him out by his harness, he had to swim up through an underground pipe.*

- On one of Hasty's first searches, he trailed to a 2½-year-old boy who had wandered five miles from the last seen point.

- Hasty helped us to rescue a little dog, whose owner had died on an icefall. The pup would not let any of the searchers get close until Hasty befriended him.

- Hasty found a woman in the bottom of a swimming pool, even after the cover had been placed over the pool.

- Hasty found an avalanche victim alive who was buried for 14 minutes.

- Hasty found many other people who had become lost in the wilderness, buried in avalanches, and drowned in lakes and rivers.

After all he had done for us, our gift of love and thanks was to let him go. After Hasty's injection on April 10, it started to snow. Dan, Sandy, and I went for a Hasty Memorial Run and thought about how the snow was symbolic of our Heavenly Father's sharing in our pain. It was appropriate that the precipitation would be snow, rather than rain, since snow was where Hasty was the most comfortable.

Hasty is survived by Sandy—his 8-year-old friend, fellow Golden Retriever and family member, Bethany—his 12-year-old human friend and family member, Rachel—his 12-year-old human friend and family member, Dan—his adult friend and family member, and Patti—his friend, family member, and SAR dog handler. He was deeply loved and will be greatly missed.

Hasty taught us many lessons, but probably the most important is that God gives each one of us a purpose in life with the gifts and talents to support it. Hasty found pure joy in searching; there was nothing as important to this "canine working machine." If each one of us could get a glimpse of why we were placed on this earth and then set our minds and hearts to accomplishing that goal, the world would be a better place.

1 Handler Preparation

I showed up for my first search dog event, an avalanche weekend at the top of Vail Pass, eager and anxious to learn as much as I could. I was immediately aware of a strange unfamiliar phenomenon—search and rescue politics. This phenomenon was not quite as apparent during the avalanche training drills. However, at the business meetings, I at first wondered whether I was made of the right stuff for this kind of work. I learned that during an organization's infancy there are many growing pains, and the handlers who are able to distance themselves from the political nonsense would have an easier time staying in for the long haul.

> Many highly skilled dog handlers have abandoned SAR because they were unable to develop the thick skin necessary for dealing with political quagmires.

I firmly recommend that people approach their initial encounters with search and rescue dog training "dog-less." This enables them to learn the fundamental SAR lessons, unencumbered by puppy antics. In my experience, while I was waiting for Hasty to be born, I had a "leg up" as I observed many breeds—canine and human. I was able to make decisions in a much more objective manner.

Try to read this book and attend SAR dog schools with an open mind. Do not be afraid to admit that this one aspect of dog training might not be "your thing." Avalanche dog handling is not for everyone.

None of us realizes, when we decide to work a search dog, the major enterprise upon which we are embarking. With a bright-eyed, Polly Anna attitude, we may remark: "this will be really good for my dog," or "won't it be fun to spend so much time with my dog doing something we both enjoy?" Sobering reality strikes harshly the first time we stare into the face of a young person who, with little warning, has left the world of the living to become one more statistic buried in the path of the 'white plague.' At this point, unless our motivations are correct, we may decide to find a less dangerous hobby. Believe me—that's okay. Search and rescue (SAR) dog handling is not for everyone.

Takes All Kinds

Avalanche dog handlers tend to be a masochistic bunch. They do not mind spending hours, or even days, out in some of the worst weather imaginable. They rather enjoy frozen eyelashes, beards, and jaw-breaking energy bars. They take pleasure in the fact that their high-tech thermos keeps liquids lukewarm for three hours. I have conducted an independent study and after a great deal of research and observation, I have reached the conclusion that these idiosyncrasies correspond proportionately to the elevation of a handler's residence. You see, avalanches usually occur where there is more than a little snow and less than a little oxygen.

Copper Mountain Ski Patrol 2001-2002 With Avalanche Dogs, Sandy, Skadee, and Pager (left to right) by Cullen Lyle

Not to say that "flatlanders" cannot or should not do avalanche rescue work. There are seasons when the mountain people need all the help they can get. Nevertheless, dog handlers who live more than an hour from avalanche territory must realize that they may never search for a potentially live victim. Theirs may be the job of clean up after the hasty and early strike teams have exhausted their efforts. These handlers should have other outlets for their SAR dog passion; i.e., wilderness, evidence, water, disaster, etc. Otherwise, they should move to higher ground, where the snow has more of a tendency to slide.

A rescue dog handler must train like a professional athlete. You will need more than a few afternoons in the local gym to prepare for missions that occur five or ten miles into the backcountry in temperatures that dip below zero degrees. Your physical, mental, and emotional stamina must be every bit as tough as your canine's.

Join the Club

Each person will need to decide which team to join—be it search and rescue, ski patrol, or search and rescue dog. What good is it to progress to a high level of proficiency as an avalanche dog team only to find that no one calls you for the avalanche missions! Search and Rescue Dogs of Colorado, to which I belong, has members scattered throughout the state. Each person is required to be a member of a local search and rescue team. One of the reasons for this prerequisite is that, while SARDOC does hold quarterly statewide training weekends, a handler must also practice on a regular basis with the local group. How absurd to have a mission in a person's own county and not be dispatched because of insufficient affiliation with the responsible SAR agencies. Talk about frustrating!

Alpine Sar Dog Handler, Roger Matthews & Sar Dog, Loki, By Roger Matthews

Look for a group that has a strong mission statement, bylaws, certification standards, affiliation with local, state, and national search and rescue groups, and experienced handlers from whom you can learn. Once you step forward and persuade the members that you have a serving attitude, you will find a team willing and able to help you reach your mutual goals. It is your responsibility to convince them that you are worthy of their time and resources. You should have no problem recognizing a good team by observing the interactions between handlers as well as dogs. There is no room for territorial disputes in rescue dog work and negative attitudes should not be tolerated

> Even as I write this, I remember dozens of situations where negativism was epidemic; few people escaped unscathed. These skirmishes were always counterproductive to the volunteers, whose only desires were to work avalanche dogs and serve those in need.

If there is not a team near your home, it is incumbent on you to be a pioneer. You need to do some leg and roadwork, visiting regions where experienced handlers are willing to mentor you. Take advantage of additional outstanding resources such as search and rescue dog schools, the National Association of Search and Rescue (www.Nasar.org,) the National Avalanche School, and electronic mail lists, which specifically serve the search dog community.

> Take avalanche courses regularly. Intimidating as it sounds, you may be the most qualified safety authority on any given avalanche mission. Be well prepared for that eventuality. Know safe routes in and out, know how to dig hasty pits and identify different layers in the snowpack, and know when the risk is greater than the chance for a live recovery.

Many, many ski patrol avalanche dog handlers are not members of a local search and rescue group. I sympathize with that position. After spending a long day out in the winter environment, it is hard to contemplate a night search or rescue in similar conditions. However, we all hope and pray that when we respond to avalanche accidents, they will not be within our ski area boundaries. This being the case, patrollers who are not members of a SAR group may never have the opportunity to use their dogs on real avalanches with real burials. They set themselves up for major frustrations if they do not affiliate with the groups responsible for backcountry rescues in and out of their counties. The first handlers to respond to avalanche missions are those who are paged by their local SAR groups.

Above all else, realize that you will never find the perfect team to join. It does not exist. If it were perfect, it would cease to be after you and I joined. After all, you and I are the team.

> Effect change where plausible; and if you cannot be of assistance in remedying a situation, stay out of it and learn to keep your mouth shut.

We often forget that we are all just a troop of good-hearted volunteers, and the quickest way to show a volunteer the exit door is with a zealous dose of criticism. We would all promptly agree that our dogs need positive feedback and success during their training regiments, and yet we ignore our own instructions when interacting with fellow humans. Offer grace and forgiveness to others, and it will return to you in good measure.

> *"A gentle answer turns away wrath,*
> *But a harsh word stirs up anger."*
> *—Proverbs 15:1*

Some final words about volunteering for search and rescue; there are only a handful of professional dog handlers, and SAR dog work can become very expensive. In addition to dog food and veterinarian bills, the handler absorbs the costs of equipment, time away from work, and travel to and from training and missions.

Candidacy

Most search and rescue teams have a candidacy period built into their orientations. This preliminary step is for the benefit of the team as well as potential SAR members. Groups grow weary of training new people only to find that they do not make the grade and all of their valuable time and energy has been for naught.

Each organization should be able to produce guidelines that outline the candidacy process and expectations for new handlers. Each person, with his dog, should be required to pass a physical fitness test, which includes hiking a pre-determined distance with a pack of a designated weight, within a certain amount of time. We often hear that attitude is everything; search and rescue is no exception. It is more difficult to change a person's attitude than to teach him good technical skills. If that individual has exhibited the characteristics the group values, team members will eventually vote him in to full membership after due process.

If your goal is to work your avalanche dog with a ski patrol, most teams typically wait until a patroller has learned the essential elements of patrolling before allowing her to work with rescue dogs. Even at that point, a person may merely assist with drills; i.e., dig holes and be a subject. Once she has demonstrated a strong work ethic and legitimate motivation, there may be an opening for an assistant handler and she may be the perfect candidate.

Teams are looking for more than just dogs that want to please. They need handlers with teachable spirits and a level of commitment that keeps going even when times get tough; and believe me—they can get tougher than you could ever imagine. The dogs are usually easier to train than the handlers. Our dogs do not typically have to deal with one of humans' strongest and least desirable traits—pride. In search and rescue, arrogance can have deadly consequences and it must be nipped at the bud. The wise person is often the one who does not need to have the last word. We have much to learn from our silent canine partners.

> "He is your friend, your partner, your defender, your dog.
> You are his life, his love, his leader.
> He will be yours, faithful and true, to the last beat of his heart.
> You owe it to him to be worthy of such devotion."
> —Author Unknown

You Ought to Be Committed

Sometimes it feels that way. The level of commitment we bring to search dog handling may lead us to believe that we should be institutionalized. What other hobby do you know of that may require roughly 500 to 1000 hours a year? We learn to dread the familiar tones of our pagers. My husband, Dan, who is a SAR mission coordinator, loves to tell the story of how I once shook my pager at two in the morning, screaming, "What do you want?" Even if I could sleep through a call-out, neither of my dogs would stand for it. They have an uncanny sense when a page is imminent even before the first tone. Our inane pagers want everything we can give, and even some things that we cannot afford to give—our very lifeblood. So, be forewarned that unless you are highly committed, do not waste your time, or any one else's for that matter. Consider the cost.

> "Suppose one of you wants to build a tower.
> Will he not first sit down and estimate the cost
> to see if he has enough money to complete it?
> For if he lays the foundation and is not able to finish it,
> everyone who sees it will ridicule him, saying,
> 'This fellow began to build and was not able to finish.'"
> —Luke 14:28

The balancing act is fragile and many a dog handler has had to learn prioritization lessons the hard way. A long time ago, Dan and I decided that our family would not suffer because of search and rescue. This was not as difficult during our first four years with Hasty, since children were not yet in the picture.

Chapter 1 Handler Preparation 9

Beth And Rachel In Rocky Mountain National Park, By Dan Burnett

However, things became more complicated with the arrival of our daughters, Beth and Rachel. We found creative solutions to middle of the night calls and out of county, multiple day missions. We learned to juggle responsibilities and often this meant that Dan responded to the rescue missions and I responded to searches. I recommend that you intentionally decide where to draw the line so that your children and spouse do not resent your SAR involvement. Without Dan and the children's support, there is no way I could have committed as much of my life to rescue dog work.

Many marriages, friendships, professions, and even lives have met their demise at the search dog altar and an unhappy, unbalanced personal life can only result in an unhappy, unbalanced search and rescue career. Some of the people I respect most in SAR would have to admit that their personal lives are in shambles. Long after our beloved search and rescue canines are gone, and the cartilage has disintegrated from our knees, our families and friends will continue to be at our sides. Know when to say, "no—enough is enough." Life after search and rescue does exist…at least that's what they say.

Avalanche Specialist

Many rescue dog handlers are tempted to specialize in one aspect of search; this is especially true with avalanche dog handlers. Wilderness airscent allows dogs to use their finely tuned nose in other venues.

As with avalanche, a person lost in the wilderness constantly sloughs off minuscule scent particles. The scent can travel great distances, depending on weather conditions. The dog handler typically acquires an article of clothing that has the missing party's scent. Many dogs are trained to discriminate this scent from that of all the other searchers. The mission coordinator assigns an airscent dog team an area to search. The handler, with the assistance of a navigator, considers wind direction and terrain, and subsequently determines the best strategy to cover the sector, in order to locate the missing party. There are two ways to measure success. The team either: 1) clears an area; i.e., decides the subject is not in that particular region or 2) the team finds the missing party. Both scenarios illustrate success. Consider the reasons for adding wilderness airscent to your team's syllabus:

- Wilderness airscent is very similar to avalanche search. At an avalanche mission, the dog initially searches for scent that is in the air and follows it to its point of origin.

- An avalanche search rarely has a happy outcome for victim, friends, families, searchers, and dogs. Dogs are every bit as susceptible to depression after they locate dead bodies as are their human counterparts. Some of the dogs used at the Oklahoma City bombing never recovered from their experiences with death and dying. The good news is that the majority of wilderness subjects are found alive.

- Other SAR dog disciplines offer an opportunity to fine tune search skills. Wilderness training increases your dog's proficiency in avalanche work. There have been cases in which avalanche victims have survived the initial slide and wandered away from the deposition, only to die of exposure or injuries because of a strategic failure to expand the search perimeters. The wilderness/avalanche dog team has the training to think and smell beyond the scope of the obvious avalanche scenario.

- A dog trained in more than just avalanche rescue provides a greater resource to the emergency medical services community.

Japanese Sar Dog Team, Emiko Masuda and Audi During Winter Sar Training, By Emiko Masuda

2 Equipment

What a thrill to know that after two hours of trailing our 2-½ year old missing party, my dog, Hasty remained on task. Even grazing bulls and highway traffic could not distract him from his focused desire to lead me to the toddler, who had wandered away from his family's campsite on Kenosha Pass.

Four hours and two miles into our trail, I realized that Hasty and I had become separated from the other members of our search party. That, in and of itself,

Patti Rewarding Hasty For A Wilderness Find, By Dan Burnett

would not have concerned me so much if it were not for the fact that they had our only radio; and now I had no means of communication with mission base. I needed to let them know that I was relatively sure that we were on track and close to our runaway toddler.

Fortunately, another searcher on an A.T.V. (all-terrain vehicle) drove up behind us. They were able to radio our coordinates back to mission base, as well as the other members of my search team. The A.T.V. then drove up ahead and found the youngster, still wandering in the same direction; he was a 2-½ year old with a mission.

It is always nice when there is a happy conclusion to a potentially troublesome mission. The sense of urgencies increases with youngsters and "oldsters." Lacking necessary SAR equipment can have seriously damaging consequences. What if I had found the toddler and he had needed serious medical attention. Without a radio, I may have had to leave him to get help.

The Boy Scouts and Girl Scouts are right. "Be prepared."

There are many similarities between the backpacks for general search and rescue and avalanche dog handling. I would like to concentrate primarily on the items unique to the avalanche dog handler's cache.

Avalanche Rescue Beacons

Avalanche rescue beacons are small battery operated devices that constantly emit a signal when turned to transmit mode. If a person wearing a beacon is buried in an avalanche, the other members of the party switch their beacons to receive. By working systematic search patterns, rescuers can pinpoint the exact location of the buried victim, by finding the stronger signal as they get closer to the transmitting beacon. Probing and ensuing shoveling finally locate the buried person.

There are various methods of beacon search. Every avalanche dog handler must regularly attend avalanche courses that teach and train in the various beacon search methods.

> "Lady Luck was with a group of four back-country skier in Colorado in 1988 when three of the skiers were completely buried in a small slide they triggered. The group was well equipped, all had beacons and shovels, but only one of the members was trained and practiced in the use of an avalanche rescue beacon. Two others in the group had very limited training while the fourth had no training whatsoever. It was the fourth member who was not caught in the slide. Relying on instincts rather than the beacon, he quickly spotted a hand protruding from the snow and dug out the most experienced member who used his beacon to find the other two buried skiers. They survived, and today all four are very proficient with avalanche rescue beacons."
> —Dale Atkins, Colorado Avalanche Information Center

Despite the fact that beacons, also known as transceivers, are becoming increasingly pricey for volunteers, no avalanche dog handler should ever be without one. In fact, all members of your search party must be equipped with one. There are many excellent brands currently on the market. As with every other piece of rescue equipment, you must practice to become competent with your beacon. Without proper training, even your top of the line beacon will only benefit you if you are the one buried; it will not help you to locate another person.

> "If you go out (of bounds,) you have to do more than carry a beacon. It's not a magic crystal, it won't ward off witches or dragons; it's useless if your friends don't know how to use it."
> —Scott Toepfer, Colorado Avalanche Information Center

I have rarely placed a beacon on one of my dogs. A dog is often working while individuals are performing beacon searches, in which case you would have to turn the dog's beacon off anyway. A handler needs to ask herself whether the need for a beacon indicates that the dog is in a situation that is too risky.

Special rescue beacons exist that only transmit, if you decide you would like to place a beacon on your dog. They are compact and can be placed inside a pocket on the dog's vest. They also transmit a different sounding and timed signal, so that rescuers can distinguish the sound from that of a human's beacon. The intent is that in the case of a human and dog burial, the human would be located first. I know…you thought I was going to say the opposite. Another idea would be to train our dogs to use the beacons. Then we could just send our dogs into the field, while we stayed home and drank hot chocolate! Just kiddin'.

> When practicing, bury beacons in a plastic container so that shovels and probes do not damage them.

Practice, practice, and continue to practice with your beacon. Practice until you are able to locate another buried beacon in a matter of minutes or even seconds. It is my opinion that you can more finely pinpoint the location of the buried beacon by unstrapping your own beacon from your chest, facilitating horizontal and vertical orientation. Be aware that there may be false indications when practicing in buildings and around other electronic devices.

The difference between life and death in avalanche search is a matter of seconds. As a dog handler, you may think that you will not have to use a beacon or probe poles…think again. I was practicing with our SAR team for a Mountain Rescue Association re-accreditation, and I ended up working my dog, being hasty search team leader, and performing a beacon search simultaneously. You just never know.

To make your practice interesting, race to see who can locate the buried beacon first—the human searcher or the dog. This can be a fun trick to impress other SAR and patrol group members.

Leash & Collar

Perhaps this should go without saying, but never, ever be around helicopters or moving vehicles without a leash.

> A leash in your pack may save your dog's life. Consider the risks to your dog and other rescuers: helicopter blades, cliffs, highways, and aggressive dogs.

Never use a training (choke or pinch) collar while working a SAR dog. Training collars are for walks and obedience training—period. A dog running through the woods while wearing a training collar can easily become a hung dog. Myriad of small branches can simply ensnare your unsuspecting canine. Buckle collars make far better sense.

Wands

Most SAR teams have red, blue, and yellow wands in their hasty search packs to mark the areas probed, safe routes in and out, and clues. Each dog handler should carry special wands that are a color unique from the hasty search wands. I use florescent flagging marked with the words "Dog Alert." These flags are helpful in strategizing the placement of probe lines. In cases where the victim has been buried more than 15 to 20 feet, we have been able to return during the spring thaw to locate the victims close to the dog's initial alert wands.

> Marked wands will increase your credibility with the local SAR or ski patrol agency. Label each one with your name and telephone number.

Collapsible Probe Poles

We like to think that as dog handlers, we will not have to use those nasty, long steel or metal poles. If you have ever probed, you know that of which I speak. It is not easy! After a full day of probing, every muscle in your arms and back ache, and your hands are cold and wet. However, there will be times when you may have to perform this difficult task; be prepared. Just once and you will have a

Sue Purvis, Crested Butte and Sardoc Handler, shoveling to a Probe "Strike," By Chris Ladoulis

greater appreciation for all the people willing to stand in perfect lines, probing and advancing so meticulously.

> Probing is far better than digging in the wrong places. Digging should rarely occur before there has been a probe pole strike.

Skis or Snowshoes

While in most situations I prefer skis, during avalanche missions, snowshoes may be my preferred mode of transportation. Usually a dog has to accompany the handler while going in and out of the rescue site. Ideally, the team may be able to hitch a ride into the slide on a helicopter, snowmobile, snowcat, chairlift, or toboggan. However, it is getting out of the field that may be a problem.

> Never get in a helicopter and assume the luxury of a round-trip flight. In fact, plan to travel out of the field independently. Carry sufficient survival gear for this eventuality.

Snowshoes are usually slower and they compress the snow better than skis, to reduce the amount the dog has to post hole. Obviously, if you can solicit a ride for your dog out of the field, you are in luck. In that eventuality, you would be glad to have brought skis. Unfortunately, we usually do not have that kind of information before heading into the field.

> Serious avalanche dog handlers are efficient and skilled in various modes of backcountry transportation. They should never be a liability to the rescue operation.

Warm Clothing

We go to all kinds of trouble to ensure that our dogs have coats and dispositions suitable to the cold environment. Are we as prepared as our furry buddies? I have been on searches where rescuers could not fulfill their assignments because of insufficiently warm clothing. I hate to admit it, but ski patrollers can be some of the worst offenders. We are sometimes not as conditioned as our SAR associates to spending a full day or night out in the cold; Patrol Headquarters is usually a mere chairlift ride or two away. Figure out the types of layering that will work for you in diverse scenarios. Obviously, most avalanches occur during, or shortly after, extreme wind and/or snow events. Train in all weather conditions so that there are no surprises when the real thing comes around. Do not become the weak link in your finely tuned SAR machine. Not only will you be letting your victim and team down; you will be disappointing your dog.

> Paramo makes great clothing systems. Find the manufacturer and combination of clothing articles that suit your particular needs and wants.

Avalanche Shovel

Shoveling is another task we would like strike from the dog handler's job description. Not so, not so. Those shovels are for more than just snow. Good etiquette in the backcountry, and especially at the ski areas, demands that canine deposits be conveyed to the closest tree well. Sometimes when Hasty had to answer nature's call, patrollers would joke, "Haste makes waste." Get it? A dog handler's avalanche shovel will probably be more utilized than any other on the ski patrol or rescue group team. You will dig more snow caves and bury more people than you would care to guess. However, not to worry...it is all a part of your finely tuned personal fitness plan.

> Get a telescoping, metal scoop shovel. The small plastic avalanche shovels crack and break in real deposition.

Radios

An avalanche drill should never be conducted without at least two radios. Too much can potentially go wrong and a radio is your only communication link with buried subjects. Invest in a few programmable radios if you are not part of a group that has radios you can use.

Radio check to verify subject is okay. By Cullen Lyle

> Suitable radios are available through your SAR or Ski Patrol group. If you belong to the team, you will usually not have to purchase your own.

Water and Dog Bowl

We have no problem remembering extra water for our dogs when the temperatures are sweltering and our own thirst prompts us to water our dogs. However, we overlook the fact that our dogs have just as great a need to remain hydrated during winter search. I often see dogs try to quench their thirst by eating snow. Unfortunately, their efforts are in vain for they are not able to access enough water in this manner to make a significant difference. Always carry extra water and a collapsible water bowl whenever your dog is searching or training.

> A hydrated dog's nose works significantly better then a dehydrated dog's nose.

Vaseline

Being a Golden Retriever handler, I deal with snowballs that form between my dogs' toes. So far, my best method for mitigating this problem, besides keeping their foot hair short, has been to place petroleum jelly between their toes.

Strobe Light or Cyalume Sticks

It is unusual to work avalanche missions during the night, but sometimes we have no choice. When working in the dark, it is helpful to have some type of illumination on our dogs. Before the strobe bike lights became available, I placed chemical cyalume sticks on Hasty's harness. The advantage of the strobe lights is that they are more visible and the batteries last for a long time, while the Cyalume sticks are only good for about eight to twelve hours. Another alternative is multi-colored electronic laser sticks that last about twelve hours. See the Appendix Resources section for website locations. Some type of illumination is also valuable for those unlikely scenarios where teams have to enter or leave the field before dawn or after dark. Lights or sticks can easily be attached to either the dog's collar or harness.

First Aid Kit

The gear in your avalanche first aid kit is not very different from your regular dog and human supplies. Super Glue is indispensable for nasty ski cuts, as are bandages and dressing. I have trouble keeping booties on my dogs' feet, but regardless, I carry them for the unusual eventuality of frostbitten or badly cut feet. Every avalanche rescue worker should carry a pocket mask to perform CPR on the avalanche victim, should there be a potential resuscitation.

The following is a general list of recommended first aid supplies:
- Bandaging (gauze wrap & vet wrap)
- Adhesive Bandages
- Cake Decorating Gel Tube (for instant glucose)

- Dog Booties
- Dressing (4 x 4s)
- Ladder Splint
- Medical Tape
- Nasal Airway
- Oral Airway
- Pocket Mask
- Rubber Gloves
- Super Glue
- Trauma Scissors
- Triangular Bandages
- Tweezers

GPS, Compass, Maps

We often fail to recognize the importance of navigational tools, in the field of avalanche search. Occasionally, you may have to guide yourself into and out of the field. A good grasp of orienteering, as well as the use of maps, compasses, and global positioning systems (GPS) may be helpful for marking alerts in an especially large slide. A good practical skills book is *GPS Made Easy: Using Global Positioning Systems in the Outdoors* by Lawrence Letham. Letham is an electrical engineer with a passion for hiking and exploring.

> GPS is able to calculate time, altitude, latitude, and longitude. The way it works is by calculating the difference in time between when a signal is sent out and when it is received. They work off satellites equipped with atomic clocks.
> —*Microsoft Encarta Encyclopedia*

Dan and Sandy doing some meaningful male bonding, by Joe Willett

Great Husband

...Or wife! Sorry, my husband told me I had to put that. I did, just to see if he would read the book again. Seriously, nothing can turn a great avalanche team sour quicker than a family that resents the handler's involvement with SAR. In our early days, Dan spent nearly as much time as I did digging holes, being buried, and shoveling. Training an avalanche dog requires a team effort: you will need help. It is all about support.

> Any significant endeavor is more meaningful if there is someone special with whom to share defining moments and highlights.

3 Puppy Selection

Mickey was the fifth patroller to ski cut Graveline after explosive intervention had seemingly little effect on the starting zone. Fellow patrollers watched as nearly the entire bowl enveloped Mick, carrying him almost 1500 feet. He was found quickly by a rescue beacon search, standard equipment for all patrollers on snow safety routes.

During a technical debriefing, we concluded that someone without a beacon buried as deeply as Mickey, would not be located for a long, long time. Thus began our research on alternative means of avalanche search.

I visited other ski areas and SAR groups, observing their training programs and the ways different dog breeds worked. We raised the money to purchase our first dog through the Copper Mountain Chapel. Mountain Education Fund. The fund has continued to fund avalanche and medical training and equipment over the years since its inception.

Hasty working an introductory avalanche problem, By Dave Weissman

I cannot over-emphasize the importance of starting out on the right foot with a good puppy. Do not take the puppy selection phase casually. There are important decisions to make regarding the breed, gender, bloodlines, and temperament. Observe a multitude of dogs, and confer with breeders, SAR dog handlers, and veterinarians. There is no substitute for being patient and making an informed decision. There are so many traits to look for and yet each one of major significance. Ultimately, the dog I want for SAR is:

- Structurally sound and athletic, with good stamina and agility…yet never a threat to people or other canines,
- Driven to work…yet always willing to please,
- Well socialized…yet curious and adaptable,
- Loyal…yet independent,
- Playful…yet intelligent,
- Obedient and trainable…yet stubborn, and
- Spirited…yet disciplined.

He has been gifted with a:

- Prey instinct,
- Superior nose,
- Strong work ethic,
- Gift for public relations, and he is the
- Dog you will love for the rest of his life.

> Investing in a good puppy is money well spent. Even if your time is wholly a voluntary labor of love, no one could ever pay you enough for your SAR dog.

I selected a Golden Retriever breeder and was much like an expectant mother, anxiously awaiting the arrival of her first child. We had decided his name would be Hasty. On search and rescue missions, the hasty team is the first strike crew sent rapidly into the field, in hopes of saving lives.

Being my first rescue dog, I chose a male alpha dog. I rationalized that, since I was new to SAR dog handling, I needed a dog that, knowing he was right, had the stamina and moral fortitude to resist when I tried to pull him off a scent. This proved to be the case when…

One summer evening, we responded to an outdoor swimming pool from which a woman had disappeared earlier that day. The pool attendant remembered seeing her in the early afternoon, lounging on the pool deck. When it started to get dark, her worried husband dialed 911. Her belongings were still in the locker-room, and all she had was the bathing suit in which she was swimming. The pool attendant had already cleaned the bottom and placed the cover over it for the night. All indicators pointed to foul play. Fire rescue personnel scoured the ditches along the roads near the last seen point, while SAR members searched adjacent swamps and bike paths.

We arrived at the pool at 10:00 p.m. and scented Hasty on the missing woman's clothes that we had retrieved from out of her locker. He tracked to the door that entered the pool area. As we opened the door, I noticed that the steam from under the pool cover blew directly into our faces. Hasty picked up his nose and proceeded to walk out onto the cover, immediately falling into the water. It is useful to receive occasional reminders that our dogs do not walk on water.

I was mortified! There we were, under the scrutiny of the local detectives, police, and fire chiefs —a politically bad time for Hasty to be messing around. How could he humiliate me at such a time! I decided it was best to try again, so we went back;

and, this time, I scented him on the towel at her lounge chair. He gave me a perfect instant replay.

After pulling Hasty out of the pool again, we removed the pool cover and discovered that the water was extremely murky because of filtration problems. We called water rescue, which sent a diver to the bottom. He, in due course, located the missing woman in the middle of the pool.

Had I selected a more submissive dog, I often wonder whether he would have had the resolution to continue, knowing that I disapproved of his "shenanigans" during this particular scenario. Hasty's strong will was often a source of dismay and frustration to me; but more often than not, I was grateful that in my naivete, he was able to solve the mystery with his strong drive and determination.

Ten-week-old sar dog, grace, testing her preliminary scentabilities, by Vi Hummel-Carr

Dominant or Submissive?

As with humans, every dog temperament has its own list of character strengths and flaws. While not to extremes, I have had personal experience with both slightly more dominant and slightly more submissive dogs. I cannot tell you whether a more dominant or more submissive dog will work best for you. Ultimately, each handler must make this decision for herself.

Select a breeder who will allow you, within certain boundaries, to perform multiple tests on the perspective puppies at different ages. I have found the Volhard aptitude test to be excellent. You can pull up a test on the web by searching for Volhard Puppy Aptitude Test. Select a testing site that is unfamiliar to the puppies and free of distractions. The various categories included are social enticement, desire to follow, confinement, social dominance, elevation dominance, retrieving, touch sensitivity, sound sensitivity, sight sensitivity, and structure. The scoring is one to six for each section: one being the most dominant and aggressive and six being the most independent and uninterested in people.

With my current dog, Sandy, the breeder and I performed tests on the litter independently and concurred that the same puppy met the desired criteria. Two sets of eyes are always better than one. Hasty consistently scored mostly 2's, while Sandy was mostly 3's. Hasty was a little more confident in his SAR work, while Sandy has been an easier dog to live and work with. If in doubt, a puppy that falls in the middle is probably a safe bet for most handlers. The more experienced you are with SAR, the more flexibility you have to move either direction from the middle.

Other factors to consider when observing litters are the puppy's energy levels. I look for a puppy that continues playing when all the littermates have run out of steam and sacked out. I also experiment with the puppy's interest in using its nose by hiding a dirty sock upwind of the play area to see whether it is tractable to following scent.

Once you have exhausted all the wonderful testing resources, the determining vote may ultimately come down to a gut feeling. Something about that little ball of fuzz, something that you cannot describe, grabs hold of your heart and you know that you cannot live another day without it. You count the days until you can finally make this puppy a full-fledged member of your family.

Male or Female

There are SAR dog handlers who will only work with male dogs and others who swear by females. On the ski patrol and with our SAR group, we generally have a good mixture of both genders. Initially, I chose a male because, as a novice dog handler, I wanted a stronger-willed animal. This is not to say that females do not have powerful wills. However, within the Golden Retriever breed, it has been my experience that the males tend to be more self-confident and assertive than the females. Both genders do great avalanche work and gender is often a personal preference issue.

A factor requiring serious consideration is whether to alter an avalanche dog. My inclination is to neuter or spay a dog, and at a young enough age that he does not scent mark and is less aggressive—preferably before six or nine months of age. The handler should make a choice between whether she is going to have a breeding program or a SAR dog program. It is extremely difficult to do both. Some might call this a conflict of interests.

Female and male dogs alike frequently distract an intact dog from his focus. Waiting until Hasty was two years old was a mistake because he never lost his penchant for scent marking, and few things are more exasperating than waiting while the male avalanche dogs mark all the same places on the deposition. I believe that the time and energy expended in marking, significantly diminishes the dog's effectiveness. I would rather have a dog that gains his sense of satisfaction from how well he searches, than from how large an area he marks. I guess it would not be a problem if all the dogs knew that the only place they could mark was the location of the victim. Unfortunately, it is not usually that simple.

Further reasons to spay and neuter your SAR dogs:

For dogs

- Reduces roaming.
- Prevents testicular and prostate cancer.
- Reduces aggression with other dogs and people, as well as mounting.

For bitches

- Reduces risk of breast and uterine cancer when performed before the first two cycles.
- Prevents serious infections of the uterus, unplanned litters, and false pregnancies.
- Prevents the need to keep the bitch away from training sessions during heat cycles.

Pure-Bred or Mixed

Excellent question. SAR dog handlers have had success with both mixed and purebred dogs. Some excellent rescue dogs have been saved from the local pound. However, take care that you do not inherit someone else's mistreatment or negligence. With abuse and neglect come health and temperament problems that may linger for the remainder of the dog's life. It may take more effort and time than you have, trying to reverse the trauma that has been inflicted on the poor victim. That said, some of the best search dogs I know are of the "Heinz 57" variety.

An advantage of buying from a kennel is that you get a bloodline history. I always want to know whether the parents are OFA (Orthopedic Foundation of Animals) hip certified, are clear of epilepsy and cancer, and have good eyes and strong hearts. Arnold

Schwarzenegger once said that the best way to insure success in bodybuilding is to select your parents very carefully! Obviously, people do not have this prerogative. However, we do have the ability to choose the parents of our SAR dogs. A kennel that supplies puppies to other working dog handlers develops a reputation for producing structurally, mentally, and emotionally sound animals. Observing the sire and dam frequently provides a good illustration of the puppy's size and characteristic traits.

Even with health contracts from the kennel, there are no guarantees. At two years of age, after Hasty had certified in both avalanche and wilderness, I received his OFA results. I was very disappointed to discover that his hips were moderately dysplastic. To watch him move and work, no one, not even our veterinarian, would have guessed it. The breeder said that she would be happy to replace him; obviously, that was not an option. Hasty was my partner and I would never trade him in like some used car. He continued to work beautifully with little clinical signs of dysplasia until his last year of life. As you can see, hip dysplasia does not necessarily disqualify a dog for SAR work.

> It is possible to have preliminary hip and elbow x-rays read by the OFA at the age of six months. Though they will not issue a certificate for a dog under two years of age, it is helpful to know how a young dog is developing structurally. PennHipp is another method for early diagnosis. Through this vehicle, International Canine Genetics has had good predictability for hip dysplasia in puppies as young as four months by studying the laxity of the hip joints.

Beware of registered dogs bred strictly for the show ring, with little thought given to working structure and health clearances. I remember years ago listening in on a heated discussion between two breeders at a SAR dog school. They were dismayed by the state of affairs for their particular breed. Various kennels had resorted to producing two different bloodlines: one for working dogs and one for show ring dogs. The dogs that did well in conformation could not navigate an obstacle course to save their lives. They were not the athletes that we require for search and rescue work. I know handlers who have had to start new SAR dogs every few years because of structural faults.

> There are many potentials at your local animal control and in certain breed's rescue system. Yes, you are giving these abandoned canines a second chance, but for how long? You have very little knowledge of their health history or primary foundation. Many of these dogs were relinquished because they were uncontrollable or were owned by people who did not understand the intricacies of the breed.
>
> At least by purchasing a SAR prospect from a reputable and responsible breeder, you know that necessary health screenings have been performed before ever breeding the sire and dam. It is far less risky having your bundle of fuzz during its primary development stages. There is tremendous potential for letting ghosts out of the closet when an older rescued dog is placed under stress.
>
> Make it a priority to visit with both the sire and dam of the prospective litter. Determine whether you like what you see in terms of temperament and structure. More importantly, do some research and try to connect with the grandparents of these puppies. There is a proven association between the temperament and health of the grandparents and the second generation.
>
> Do some groundwork and see if you can find older puppies from either of the parents or grandparents in question to determine if you like what you see in terms of working ability. Has this breeding produced other working dogs; i.e., SAR, detection, obedience, hunting, or other sports?
>
> —Kim Gilmore, SAR Dog Handler with Flathead County SAR, North Valley SAR, and 1st Special Response Group

The winds gusted more than 70 miles an hour the morning of January 11, 1987 on Pearle Pass. If not for a 38-year old woman and her black lab buried in an avalanche, no one in their right mind would have ventured into the backcountry. Our search was in terrain completely above timberline at 13,000 feet, and the temperatures were between minus 10 and 20 degrees, with wind loading exponentially increasing the avalanche hazard and risk for the rescuers. Every now and then, I would see a gust of wind nearly pick up 75-pound Hasty and carry him across the debris.

Sandy searching in typical inclement weather, By Jeff Sparhawk

Half way through our search I realized that one of the other avalanche dogs was lethargically stumbling over the medium sized slabs of snow. When I got to him, I noticed that he was shaking uncontrollably. Max snapped uncharacteristically at the rescuers who tried to help him. His thin coat was insufficient for that day's weather demands, and he had to be evacuated before he reached a critical state of hypothermia.

That was his last avalanche mission. Some dogs are built for the desert and some dogs are built for the snow.

SAR dog bloodhound, Stella, running a trail, By K.C. Harmon

Which Breed

The uninitiated might expect the avalanche dog to be a large St. Bernard, a keg of brandy dangling from its neck. Others might anticipate a Bloodhound dragging a struggling Inspector Clousseau-type character. I have never seen a St. Bernard at an avalanche mission, and only one Bloodhound. Avalanche debris is difficult to navigate. The dogs we select for avalanche work are typically sporting, herding, or working dog breeds; i.e., Australian Shepherds, Border Collies, Chesapeake Bay Retrievers, German Shepherds, Golden Retrievers, and Labrador Retrievers. They must have good noses, heavy undercoats, and strong athletic structures. Of course, within each breed there are significant differences.

> "Although avalanche dogs have been used in Europe to locate victims buried by snow avalanches since the early 1940s, history relates that rescues have been going on for more than 200 years. Rescue operations, as we know them today, were revived in about 1939.
>
> The most famous St. Bernard "Barry," named by the brothers of the St. Bernard Hospice, saved 41 lives in the Swiss Alps about 1810. He was an avalanche dog as well as a search dog and found people who were lost and exhausted while trying to cross the snow-covered Alps between Italy and Switzerland during winter. Barry even found his handler, Brother Julius of the Hospice who was buried in an avalanche while trying to rescue travelers. However, it was too late, he was already dead.
>
> Today, Barry would probably not be recognized as a St. Bernard. Although he weighed approximately 80 pounds he was not the shaggy, flap-lipped type we are accustomed to seeing. He was a trim, short-haired dog, with the reddish-brown and white coloring of the traditional St. Bernard."
> —"Capabilities & Limitations of Avalanche Dogs," 1981
> Willy J. Grundherr, California Rescue Dog Association

SARDOC Handler, Marcia Mcmahon and her Newfoundland, Yeti, preparing to do some wilderness airscent training, By Roger Matthews

Realize that different breeds work avalanche SAR differently. I have marveled at the methodical nature of the German Shepherds, compared to the random nature of the Golden Retriever's search. Some of the herding dogs, Border Collies and Australian Shepherds, have a greater tendency to watch their handlers for direction than the self motivated Labrador Retrievers. Take the time to observe different breeds at work before deciding which one suits you best.

Winter Coats

Heavy coats are essential. Double coats are better for cold, wet conditions inherent to avalanche search conditions. The outer coat, with its harsh guard hairs, acts as a moisture barrier. You can put booties and coats on your dog for colder weather, but those articles will often hinder the dog's ability to work and dig. Once a dog becomes cold, its focus turns to survival rather than work. Am I suggesting that Nordic dogs that stay outside and sleep in the snow would be the answer? Don't get too excited yet.

Off Lead

Avoid dogs that do not work well off lead. Avalanche debris is no place to be attached to a four-wheel-drive canine. The dog must have the freedom to move, which is not enhanced by dragging around a handler. Hence, the difficulty in working Bloodhounds for avalanches. I am not saying that it cannot be done; it is, however, more difficult. This is also a problem for a majority of the Nordic dogs. They have been bred to run and pull in a harness, not to search with their noses off lead.

Air-scenting

It is unusual to have the advantage of a trail that leads to an avalanche victim. Therefore, it is more desirable to use a dog that wants to work the air and wind, rather than a trail. The Bloodhounds do a beautiful job of following tracks, but placing their noses in the air to follow wind-borne scent is not one of their strong suits.

Temperament

Aggressive dogs are usually too much of a headache to their handlers. An avalanche dog handler can expect to transport and work in close proximity with other dogs, with multi-faceted distractions. Dogs that become possessive of a "find" they have made will make it difficult for other dogs to confirm an alert. Overly dominant or submissive dogs may be less effective because their minds are focused on the antics of the other dogs. Avoid breeds that indicate dog aggression as an aspect of their standard.

Does One Size Fit All?

It is doubtful. We have held a number of avalanche dog schools at Copper Mountain over the years. Handlers showed up with Standard Poodles, Newfoundlands, Burmese Mountain Dogs, Rottweilers, Labs, Shepherds, Goldens, etc. It was interesting watching one of the handlers try to get his large, actually extra large, Newfie on the chairlift. After three attempts, we scrapped the operation. Trapper was banished to the Lower Patrol Room, where he spent the remainder of the day. Imagine how difficult it would be to try to load a helicopter with a dog larger than 100 pounds. Besides the weight limits, there are certain space constraints. Another consideration is whether a particular breed has the agility to maneuver around large chunks of avalanche debris and through breakable snow.

It is not the intent of this book to breed bash, and the unconventional breeds are nearly all possible to train for avalanche. I have seen all shapes, sizes, and colors of dogs perform avalanche work. Nevertheless, be responsible enough to make an informed decision. If you select a non-conformist breed for avalanche work, be prepared to spend more time than might be necessary with other breeds. Would you rather get a dog to certification in one to two years or three to four? Find a dog that is bred to do what you want—use its nose and brain, dig, survive in the cold, and work for humans. It all comes down to whether you can trust a particular dog with the demands unique to avalanche search.

Tasha, Crested Butte and SAR Dog, operational in wilderness airscent and avalanche
Photo By Chris Ladoulis

I had decided to wait to get another puppy until Hasty retired. However, I discovered that things do not always work out the way I plan. We were hosting an Avalanche Dog School and during the opening session, people were introducing themselves, explained what they wanted to get out of the classroom and field sessions. Sandy McFarland, who came without a dog, stood up and explained that she had seen an article about Copper's dog program in her local newspaper. She wanted to study the dogs, see which qualities made for a good avalanche dog, and donate one of her puppies to our program. I had observed Sandy's dogs at an exhibition and admired their obedience, athletic structure, and passion for working. We waited for our puppy to be born. Meanwhile....

On July 9, 1994, our family was attending the Mountain Community Fair and Rodeo when a sheriff's officer approached us with disturbing news. He carefully explained that our friends, helicopter pilot Gary McCall and flight nurse Sandy Sigman, were evacuating an injured woman from Mount Huron. During their landing approach, the scree on which the skids rested shifted slightly, causing the rotor to hit the mountainside. Rather than risk the lives of the patient and SAR personnel on the ground, Gary decided to pull the helicopter away from the mountain. In the process, both he and Sandy were immediately thrown out of the ship and killed.

Sandy was a dear friend and the Copper Mountain MVP of the Year the previous ski season. She was a person who knew the value of treating her patients with love as she looked into their faces while treating life threatening injuries and illnesses.

Our emergency medical service's community was devastated with the loss of two such vital lives.

The very same day that this tragedy struck, our puppy was born. I had plenty of names picked out for him: Fisher, thinking he would be a fisher of men. Dan thought Help would be a *good name so that when we were out searching and a lost person called for 'help,' our dog would come to his rescue. Needless to say, we had no choice at this point. His name would be Sandy in honor of our friend and associate. Sandy McFarland, of Timberee Goldens, generously donated a wonderful male to us seven weeks later. Hasty, never much of a player, learned to romp with Sandy and a close friendship developed. Before long, Hasty was showing Sandy the SAR ropes.*

Regardless, no dog would ever take Hasty's place.

Dog Number Two, Three, Four...

Despite the fact that SAR handlers make most of their mistakes on dog number one, no subsequent dog ever takes that first dog's place. Don't even try. Expect each of your dogs to have a unique personality, working style, and temperament. The great thing is that with each successive puppy that you handle in SAR, it becomes easier. You are already aware of those qualities from your first dog you would like to duplicate as well as the traits you would like eliminated.

I was glad that I had the opportunity to work Hasty and Sandy together for nearly four years. It was especially insightful to watch them work wilderness simultaneously. The old man would use his head, conserving energy, while the young pup would run helter-skelter. With avalanche, if Sandy was not digging as hard or fast as I thought he should, I would bring Hasty in, and the competition would begin.

> "I took her, my dog, for my teacher, and obeyed her, For she was wiser than I, and she led me back, the poor dumb beast, Like a God-sent and God-obeyed angel, To human nature, to mercy, to self-sacrifice, to belief, To worship, to pure and wedded love."
>
> —Taken from *Water Babies,* by Charles Kingsley

4 Training

"How can you get them to ride the chairlifts like that?" is a common question from the Copper Mountain guests. Getting them on the lifts is easy; they love it and probably ride the lifts better than many of the skiing public. It all has to do with thorough training and socialization. Keeping them off the lifts is another issue.

Swiss SAR dog handler, Marcel Meier with his German Shepherd in a tram in the Swiss Urner Boden Region, By Dan Burnett

When Hasty was about nine months old, he decided to get on a lift by himself. I loaded the chair behind him, begging him to stay. "If you ever stayed, stay now," I yelled up to him. I would love to have a picture of the lift operator's expression at the top unloading terminal, when he saw Hasty jump off the chair by himself.

When Can I Start?

Start right away, but watch the level of demands placed upon your puppy. If the breeder is agreeable, week seven is the ideal time to transfer attachment from the dam and litter to the new owner. Research has shown that the strongest time to influence a dog's temperament is from three to twelve weeks of age. This is a critical period for SAR dog handlers to imprint in the puppy's mind that its entire purpose in life is search. Keeping this in mind, do not forget that a young dog has many physical, mental, and emotional limitations, and a wise handler will proceed with care.

Many people wonder whether it is effective to begin with an older dog for SAR training. Yes and no. While it may work, ask yourself whether it is the optimal choice. An older dog probably has certain habits and motivations that are not effectual to avalanche search. The dog may have already developed particular patterns and motivations that will be difficult to replace with rescue work. A younger dog will retain its earliest lessons more readily than an older dog. Last, but not least, the later a dog begins training, the shorter its SAR working life. With so much of your time, energy, and finances invested in this pursuit, why settle for a career of six years, when it could be ten years. Starting a mature dog is usually not the ideal scenario.

Obedience

While an avalanche dog does not necessarily have to heel in perfect position and perform a polished finish, it is important that the dog has basic obedience skills. Enroll the puppy in a class where you can teach it to reliably and consistently stay and come. During these classes, you will develop a relationship of trust with your dog, as well as provide early opportunities for socialization with various situations, people, and dogs.

Swiss SAR dog handler, Axel Budde, prepping his young dog for wilderness work, By Dan Burnet

> "Studies have shown conclusively that the first sixteen weeks of a dog's life are of vital importance in determining his later behavior as an adult."
> —Taken from *The Art of Raising a Puppy*, p. 19
> by the Monks of New Skete

I am a strong advocate for positive training and one of the best programs I have used is "Super Puppy," out of Escondido, California. They recommend that classes begin as soon as the pup comes home from the kennel. The use of obstacles and treats teaches control and fun. You will find that the association begun in puppy training builds a strong foundation for all higher SAR education.

> Harsh training methods such as yelling and jerking on a training collar have no place in puppy obedience. When the instructions are short, fun, and rewarding, the dog becomes a much more eager learner. His enjoyment during obedience will carry over to the search and rescue disciplines. I know; I have tried both methods.

As we were performing a sweep at the end of the day, Hasty and I came upon a skiing snowman. Now, we see some unusual sights at Copper Mountain, but this was a new one for us. There was Denver Bronco, John Elway, one of the most winning quarterbacks in NFL history, shooting a commercial for the ski resort on one of the back trails. It was a steep trail at that, especially for a football player.

I was so glad that Hasty did not see this famous snowman as a threat. I would never have forgiven him if he had decided to sack John Elway, taking a bite out of one of those multimillion dollar hands.

Socialization

Spend hours familiarizing your young SAR dogs with as many objects, sensory stimulants, and situations as possible. Take them everywhere you go. In a safe and unthreatening environment, teach them to accept all types of people—big and small, male and female, with and without hats, clean-shaven or bearded, carrying a stick or without. Your goal is to raise a non-discriminating dog. They must also be able to conduct themselves responsibly around all types of dogs—giant and toy, fixed and intact, dominant and fearful, brindled and plain. They must be adept at comprehending both human and canine body language.

> "Events that occurred at a certain stage of a puppy's life affected its development more than if they had happened at other times. Though somewhat ambiguous as to precisely how many of these periods there are, they (researchers John L. Fuller and John Paul Scott) singled out as most important, the period between three and twelve weeks of age, the critical period of socialization, when a puppy has certain social experiences that exert the maximum

> influence on its future personality and temperament."
> —Taken from *The Art of Raising a Puppy*,
> pages 22-23, by the Monks of New Skete

While traveling to a NASAR convention, where we were scheduled to speak, we were involved in a two-car accident that nearly totaled our car. Sandy was in the back of the station wagon at the time. After I made sure that Dan and I were okay, I turned around to see Sandy completely unruffled. His tail wagged expectantly, wondering what kind of an amusement park ride or playground obstacle we were going to endeavor next.

Your goal should be to develop a dog that does not avoid new situations. They should be so well bonded and trust you to so implicitly that when startling and unusual scenarios arise, they know that you will be there for them. The hours you invest closely supervising a puppy's socialization will have far-reaching consequences in your SAR dog's career. This is also a crucial period for developing a tenacious bond between handlers and their rescue dog.

Praise & Rewards

Before beginning training, the handler must understand an essential component of each drill—praise. When rewarding an avalanche dog, there is no room for inhibitions. I used to scoff at handlers who acted crazy, waving their arms and screaming with a high-pitched voice. Then I saw how those "crazy people's" dogs watched their handlers every minute. They never knew what to expect. Sandy Bryson has been known to say that a dog handler should "Get down and get dirty with her dog." Because most of the people you find in avalanches are dead, it becomes a challenge to discover creative ways to praise your dog's performance in front of tired searchers, inquisitive media, and grieving family members. Save most of the animation for training drills. During actual missions, such luxuries do not exist.

Find the object that drives your dog insane. For some it will be a Frisby or ball, for others it may be a tug or squeaky toy. Whatever the reward, use it every single time you train, and do not use it for any other activity. Ski patrollers have an inexhaustible supply of gloves. Skiers and snowboarders just can't seem to hold on to their clothing and they have an uncanny propensity for spreading it out in a variety of locations—the woods, bathrooms, cafeterias, parking lots, you name it. The great thing about gloves is that our avalanche victims usually have one or two. The disadvantage of using gloves is that our dogs try to steal people's gloves as a clue to their handlers that it is about time to dust off the avalanche shovel. Gloves are better than balls for avalanche work because they do not roll down the hill.

Loki, never too tired for one more frisby retrieve, By Roger Matthews

> A novice avalanche dog handler should never take the matter of motivation lightly. Avalanche missions can last anywhere from 15 minutes to two weeks. An unmotivated dog makes for a poor companion during an extended search.

For some dogs, finding an appropriate reward is more of a challenge. Handlers often tell me that because their dog does not enjoy tugging, chewing, or retrieving, their reward is physical play and

Patti tugging with Hasty. By Dave Weissman.

hugs. That type of reward may work initially, but handlers usually find that, with time, the dog loses the motivation to continue working when a tangible reward does not exist.

You may have to exhaust the shelves of your local pet stores, but it is well worth the effort. Keep trying until you find the right "carrot" for your particular dog. However, please understand that your principle reinforcement should not be food. Food can become a tremendous distraction for a dog that works alongside other searchers who scatter food around an avalanche site', and search bases are rife with human goodies courtesy of the Salvation Army. Do not give your dog one more excuse for not focusing on its main goal, which is to find people—not food.

Spending a small amount of time training with the Swiss, I was surprised to find that they often use food as the reward. It is good to keep an open mind to new training techniques. While I would not recommend that we all go out and buy Swiss sausages, our European counterparts have convinced me that there may be a place for intermittent food rewards—especially with a dog that has grown stale and needs extra motivation.

The very best reward eventually becomes the actual act of finding. We humans are slow to attach such esoteric emotions to our canine companions, and yet I do believe that they are capable of deriving pleasure and enjoyment from search work.

> "An exercise that the dog performs cheerfully, yes, even with fervor, will have the greatest stimulating effect…provided this exercise has not been spoiled for him by an incompetent and absurd approach."
> —Taken from *How to Praise Your Dog*, 1989
> Urs Ochsenbein, Swiss Disaster Dog Association &
> California-Swiss Search Dog Association

Commands

A typical house pet probably has a vocabulary of about ten words. However, some SAR handlers claim that their dogs understand as many as 50 to 70 words.

Decide which command you will use to advise your dog that it is time to work. If your dog has already begun wilderness search, use a different word for avalanche. In our case, since we use "find" for wilderness work, we use "search" for avalanche and water. I chose a word that warned the dogs that, unlike wilderness search, they were to locate a buried person…someone that was underneath.

> Avoid using your SAR commands for other applications. For example, I do not ask my dog to "find" his Frisbee. I use fetch or seek instead. There is no sense in confusing your dog with inconsistency.

Many people do not think that their dog needs different commands for other search disciplines, reasoning that he will recognize the different scenario and know that it's time to find something that is buried. I disagree. In the case of avalanches, since we do not usually use a scent article and since there are usually many searchers on the scene at missions, I want the dogs to find something totally different. Hence, I use search. My dog knows that he is looking for someone not seen or smelled above the surface.

> "I own two dogs, and they both have been trained to respond immediately to my voice. For example, when we're outside, all I have to do is issue the following standard dog command: "Here, Earnest! Here, Zippy? C'mon! Here! I said come HERE! You dogs COME HERE RIGHT NOW! ARE YOU DOGS LISTENING TO ME? HEY!!!" And instantly both dogs, in unison, like a precision drill team, will continue trotting in random directions, sniffing the ground."
> —By Dave Barry, From "Peak Performance," p. 99, M. Christine Zink, D.V.M., Ph.D.

Documentation

Purchase a three-ring notebook and begin a training log. I have included a sample in the appendix for your review and to use if you would like. Document every training session. These reports will become instrumental in helping you to evaluate what you and your dog have accomplished and to set realistic goals. Documentation is also mandatory if your training methods are ever called into question.

> I have never had to use documentation as discoverable material. People generally want to believe the best about volunteer SAR workers. However, this is no excuse for maintaining sloppy training logs and mission reports.

Another method of documentation is by way of video cam recorder. If you have access to a VCR, it is an excellent tool for reviewing you and your dog's performance. Handlers miss many subtle clues while they are working their dogs that become apparent in the warmth and quiet of a living room or training room during debriefings and critiques.

I wish he'd just tell me what he's thinking...

I would be rich if I had a dollar for every time I have thought or heard this sentiment expressed by another handler. Since we cannot see or smell what they smell, it would be nice if our dogs could just tell us what is going on in the passageways from their noses to their brains.

They do tell us, but not usually in a way that we readily understand. It's called body language and our canine partners are masters in this dialect. Our problem is that we speak to our dogs in two languages, verbal and body. We would be much more effective with our canine partners if we were able to listen more with our eyes than our ears. We would be far more effective with our dogs if we were able to answer back to them not just with our mouths, but also with our actions. Unfortunately, what we say with our mouths sometimes contradicts what we demonstrate with our mannerisms.

Imagine how confusing it must be for our dogs when they are praised for locating a dead avalanche victim, yet simultaneously they watch our sad, depressed expressions at the senseless loss of life. Our dogs are continually aware of our feelings. The dilemma then is to discover how to convince our canine partners that finding dead people is good, despite our aversion to being around the dead. I would be troubled about a handler who did not cringe each time she found another avalanche victim. However, exposure to the smell of death is one of the most valuable training tools our dogs will ever receive for progressing to even more efficient avalanche search in the future.

The key to successful avalanche dog handling is getting to know your dog so well that you recognize even the slight nuances that she exudes. After over 18 years of marriage, Dan and I know each other's thoughts and finish each other's sentences on a regular basis. Such becomes the phenomenon between SAR handlers and their dogs. We learn to read our dogs and visa versa because we have made it a practice to study each other constantly under varying circumstances.

> **Make it a priority to learn to READ YOUR DOG and communicate in such a way that he can read you.**

No one else will be able to interpret your rescue dog's communication as well as you. Your dog will become like an open book to you. You will understand that subtle alerts, rolling, scratching at the snow surface, are the dog's way of indicating that there is scent, but not as strong as at other times. You will know that when he holds his tail, if he is fortunate enough to have one, in a certain position, he is saying one thing. When it is between his legs, it means something totally different. After 12 years of working Hasty, I noticed even the slightest angle contrast and knew that occurred because of a message transmitted from his nose via his brain to his long fluffy tail. When Hasty was new to finding dead bodies, he held his normally high wagging tail lowly between his rear legs with just a slight wag. I had never experienced this behavior during training.

The winter of '93/'94 was a dry season for Summit County. Finally, we received five or six days of heavy snow, 27", accompanied by extremely high winds. The Colorado Avalanche Information Center issued a warning and ski area snow safety teams worked non-stop to stay ahead of the increasing avalanche risk. January 7 was a typical cold and windy, but sunny Colorado day. Just before noon, while checking a trail, I received the radio call that patrollers dread most. "Code 100 with one confirmed burial"—an avalanche accident. I radioed Patrol Headquarters to see if Kevin was there to respond with Hasty. Kevin, Hasty's secondary handler, immediately jumped on a snowmobile and they began searching within minutes. Meanwhile, I caught a ride up the mountain on a lift maintenance snowmobile—what a ride!

As I arrived on the scene, Kevin briefed me that Hasty had alerted in an area slightly south of where the witnesses had begun probing and digging. I continued to work Hasty, while a

Hasty searching for scent, By Jenny Hager

probe line searched his alert. Within minutes, a "strike" was achieved under about three feet of snow.

Thanks to our MVP and Physician Advisory programs, a Flight for Life nurse and ED doctor were on scene as soon as the young woman's beautiful face was uncovered. She was a 34-year-old wife and mother, involved in the medical field at a Denver hospital. A primary assessment revealed that she was not breathing, but had a nearly indiscernible, rapid pulse, despite being buried for approximately 14 minutes. There was speculation that she had a pocket of air around her face, which furnished her with precious oxygen. Sandy Sigman, a Copper Mountain MVP and Flight for Life nurse, intubated her; and in a matter of seconds, the young woman's skin became pinker as she began breathing on her own. I remember my astonishment as I watched her eyes open and saw ice crystals move on the surface of her pupils as they started to focus and track. We bagged her with high concentrations of oxygen, while transferring her to a backboard and toboggan. Flight for Life then airlifted her to the clinic. After one night of observation in a Denver hospital, the young woman was released and sent home to her family.

In our eight years of experience, Hasty had found many people who had surrendered their lives to the tons of suffocating snow. Finally, all those hours and years of sore shoulder muscles, wet gloves, and cold feet had paid off. She was alive! I still wonder whether Hasty fully recognized how thrilled I was with his magic nose.

Rescue Dog Built for Two?

Whether an avalanche dog should have multiple handlers is a topic that gets the hackles up for many rescue dog handlers. My definitive answer is "Yes and No." I would not recommend more than one handler for avalanche dogs that do not work at ski areas. However, there are situations unique to ski patrolling that demand dual handling.

Murphy's Law ordains that when "the big one" happens, the primary handler is far from where the dog is stationed, as illustrated in the previous accident. The secondary handler may have to initially respond with the dog and work her until the primary handler arrives. Ski patrollers also have a nasty habit of blowing out a knee or getting pregnant—I did both. With a backup handler, the dog need not curtail its duties just because the handler is temporarily indisposed.

Since early training requires the assistance of a helper for runaway games, it works well to have the secondary handler start learning the ropes as the helper. This person becomes the subject once the puppy has become adept at finding the master. Dual handlers have the advantage of digging holes for each other, ensuring the existence of blind training sites. Since the other handler is experienced in watching the dog, he can more objectively evaluate the training progress and skill level of both the dog and the handler. We always respond to missions with a team of at least two patrollers and a dog. It is logical that the team's prober/support person be the secondary handler. I cannot say enough for having another set of eyes

Sandy with his two handlers, Cindy Ebbert and Patti By Cullen Lyle

to watch for dog alerts, and the secondary handler gains invaluable experience.

We require that a secondary handler certify with the dog before responding to missions as the primary handler. A word of caution! When the time comes to test the dog, have the other handler far away from the testing site. With certification jitters, dogs become confused and perform less effectively when they think they have two handlers to answer to.

On the ski patrol, people who have performed successfully as secondary handler are naturals for owning and handling new puppies the next time there's an opening. These people have proven themselves responsible and ready to be a primary handler.

Another consideration in the decision to utilize dual handlers is the breed of the dog. I observed a dog at another ski area that would not run to the avalanche site with the secondary handler when he called him to work. Certain breeds are historically one-handler dogs. In my experience, this has not been the case with Goldens;

they are fickle and will usually work with anyone who treats them nice and has a biscuit.

As with any good thing, dual dog handling can be abused if taken to an extreme. There are ski areas that have "community dogs." They live at Patrol Headquarters and they do not belong to a designated person. These dogs are vulnerable to personality disorders and neglect. With no single person responsible for them, they may be under or over exercised. No designated person ensures that the dogs are up to speed with vaccinations and nutritional needs. If there is a person who generally looks after the dog and that person leaves patrol, the destiny of the dog is again up for grabs. I have heard it said that, "This dog is so well trained that we just take him to the avalanche, and put him on auto-pilot." Perhaps, but even if the dog is alerting correctly, who has the trained eye to read the dog's subtle alerts characteristic to dead victims or deep burials? Sorry to "beat a dead horse," but please use discretion when deciding whether to employ dual handlers.

Lift Evacuation

Technical rope skills are not usually essential to avalanche dog handling; however, there are a few applications. At the ski areas, dogs get up the hill primarily on chairlifts. Should a lift break down and need to be rope evacuated, the only way to remove a dog is to belay him. In 14 years, we have never had to evacuate one of our avalanche dogs, but it could happen some day. We train for that eventuality.

> In SAR, we have used our dog harnesses to up-haul civilian dogs that have fallen into mineshafts. We have never found the need to lower a dog either over a cliff or from a helicopter into a search area.

Since the odds of having to evacuate a dog are slim, we only keep one dog-rappelling harness in the Copper Mountain lower patrol room. Our dog's vests do not double as lift evacuation harnesses. However, some ski area dogs do have a rappelling system built into the vests that the dogs wear every day.

In our protocols, the dog evacuation system is up-hauled to the handler in the chair, who then places the harness on the dog. The dog's harness is clipped into the figure eight that normally holds the lift evacuation chair, and the dog is carefully lowered to the ground. The most challenging phase is getting the dog over the edge of the chair. After that, they relax. We have found rappelling to be a great confidence builder for a SAR dog team.

The other application for a harness would be searching on a steep glacier. One time, while searching for two ice climbers in Rocky Mountain National Park, a harness might have helped. In the upper portions of the glacier, the snow was so steep that I had to use crampons. It is doubtful how well Hasty was working while in this steeper region. A rope might have helped him to feel an added measure of comfort and safety.

Dan Rappelling over a cliff with Hasty, By Patti Burnett

5 Avalanche Dog Training Progression

Most avalanche dog handlers should plan on training two to three times a week during the first winter season. A diligent and consistent handler can usually cover this progression within a year. Anticipate spending one or two weeks on each step before advancing to the subsequent step.

Step 1: Runaway Games

Start runaway games on dry land, even before the snow begins to fly. Your puppy's footing is much better on the ground and there is less risk of damage to developing bones and joints.

The puppy must have the opportunity to succeed every single time it trains at this stage of the game. Leave no question in the puppy's mind that this is absolutely the greatest thing it will ever do. After all, how often can a puppy succeed in everyday life? When it chews up the leather couch? When it leaves little tootsie rolls in the corner of the family room floor? When it whines to go out in the middle of the night? A light bulb should go off in its head that it has finally hit on a way to make you smile. Finally, the puppy is the center of attention and has a purpose in life.

Every stage of avalanche dog training requires that the master/handler have a helper. The runaway games commence with the master as the subject, and the helper as the handler. Since the dog has already begun bonding with the master, it more readily wants to find that person. Once the dog conquers the task of finding its master, it progresses to finding the helper. When advancing to each successive phase, the master assumes the role of the subject.

In preparation for this step, a hole is dug in the snow about two feet deep. The helper finds a position downwind of the hole in well-consolidated snow, so that running is less difficult and injurious to the dog and helper.

Helper releasing Sandy during a runaway drill, By Patti Burnett

The helper kneels down in the snow, holding the puppy around its chest while the master teases it with a toy. Once the master has sufficiently excited the puppy, he/she runs away, wildly waving arms, screaming, and jumping into the hole in the snow. The instant that the master is out of sight, the helper releases the dog and tells it that it is time to go to work, "Go Search." Again, this is just the term that I use. Feel free to be creative, but consistent, in your selection of commands.

As the dog chases the master, the helper runs with it, encouraging all the while. Once the handler is reached, the party begins. The master and helper both play with the dog. If the dog initially lacks interest in the reward, tease with it, hiding it, running away with it, burying it—whatever it takes. Repeat this exercise a few times and then quit for the day. In all aspects of animal training, it is critical to end on a positive note. If the dog has a bad experience, take a step back to the basics and finish with a drill in which you know the dog will succeed.

> There are times when it is necessary to return to the basics, to reinforce a lesson that your dog learned weeks or even months before.

During the next training drill, begin with another runaway with the master as the victim. Once the dog has excelled at this step, advance to having the helper play the subject. Repeat this step a few times. These exercises are the building blocks upon which you will fashion all future training. Get them down solid before moving on to the next step. For some dogs, one or two weeks of runaways will be necessary; for others, only a few sessions will suffice.

Step 2: Runaways with a Dusting of Snow

For those who have not done other forms of SAR dog handling, a definition is in order at this point. The word "alert" refers to the manner dogs use to tell their handlers that they have found scent. In disaster, wilderness, cadaver, and evidence search, dogs alert in numerous ways; i.e., barking, lying down, whining, jumping, circling, etc. However in avalanche, the preferred alert is a dig.

> Just because you encourage your dog to dig in the snow, does not give him permission to turn your backyard into a putting green. Your dog will learn the difference between the acceptable practice of digging in snow and the prohibited practice of digging in dirt.

The subject, the master first, and then the helper, runs away from the dog and jumps into the same hole used in the previous drill. This exercise is much the same as the preceding one except that another helper, helper #2, is required to shovel a dusting of snow on top of the victim. The dog is released as soon as helper #2 completes this task.

The fun thing about this step of the progression is that the puppy finally has an opportunity to dig. Avalanche dogs must love to dig. There is no way around it. I have heard it said that a police K-9's reward in protection work is the bite. For avalanche dogs, an integral part of their reward is the dig. It is your job to get down on your knees next to them, and dig with your hands. Try to beat them to the victim—make an excessive game of it. While you are at it, tell them "Good dig. Good dig." They learn to associate the action of digging with the word.

> Cassidy was a super-motivated Standard Poodle from Aspen. Somehow, she could manipulate her handler and the shovelers to do all her digging so that she would not ruin her pedicure. You had to be there! Remember these are working dogs. Make them earn their chow.

Some people who are also training their dogs for disaster work may wish to incorporate a bark alert at this point, which is fine—but, do not eliminate the dig. Most dogs can do both if trained for it—no problem. I have seen dogs that will only bark and not dig. The problem is that they may start barking at the first whiff of scent. At this point, they may become so engrossed with the barking game, that they never pinpoint the scent; that is a dilemma. Concentrate first on the dig and if the bark comes later, fine.

Before moving on to the next step, repeat this exercise; but have the helper place a tarp over the subject before again throwing a dusting of snow over the tarp. Placing more and more obstacles between the subject and the dog is an excellent motivator to teach digging.

Step 3: Runaway with a Head and Shoulder Cave

At this point, dig a head and shoulder cave into the side of your original hole. The roof of the cave should be more elevated than the entryway. This feature aids in providing a more comfortable compartment for the subject and reduces the amount of snow that falls onto the subject as the dog is digging.

Implement this step by initially having the subject run away from the dog, jumping into the hole. We will call helper #2 the shoveler from this point on. Once a subject enters the hole, with head and shoulders in the cave, the shoveler covers the subject with a dusting of snow. During this step, the best position for a subject is

Head and shoulder cave, by Cullen Lyle

on his side. I notice that when I lay on my stomach, the pressure and weight of snow on my diaphragm is quite disconcerting. As with previous steps, the helper releases the dog as soon as the subject is buried.

Continue this step alternating between the master and the helper as subjects. Do not proceed to the next step until you have gradually progressed to the point where there is up to a foot of snow piled on top of the subject and the dog is aggressively and successfully digging to the subject.

As with every step in the training progression, be sure to move on to the next phase well before your dog is bored. Avalanche work should be exciting to your dog. Keep the drills short and always end on a positive note.

Step 4: Shallow, Full Body Cave

Please review the appendix "Safety Procedures for Avalanche Dog Training," which gives instructions that are more comprehensive on safely building and training with a full body cave and burial. I recommend that you have a snowpack of at least five or six feet before building a full body cave. In Colorado, with our nefarious temperature gradient snow, a shallower snowpack is not usually safe.

Dig a hole about four feet deep straight down in the snow. Then build a cave into the uphill side of the hole large enough to comfortably shelter a full size adult. Seven feet long, 2½ feet high, and 2½ feet wide is a good rule of thumb. There should be about two feet of snow over the top of the cave. Dome the roof, so that the area over the body is higher than the entryway to the cave. By having a smaller entrance, there is less likelihood of the snow falling in on the subject while the dog is digging. Since full caves are a new

Subject in a full body cave with a rescue beacon, by Patti Burnett

experience for the dogs, providing a slight ramp into the hole will be less intimidating. I like to build caves the day before a drill to allow more time for the snow to set up, increasing the strength and integrity of the cave.

Have the master again play with the dog in a position downwind of the cave. As with all the runaway problems that preceded this step, the master runs and jumps into the cave and the helper releases the dog as soon as the master is out of sight. It is essential that the helper run with the dog so that if it is afraid to go down into the cave, the helper can assist. However, do not push the dog. The master can call the dog and encourage it. If it still does not want to enter the cave, the master goes to the dog and plays with it.

If the dog had any hesitancy entering the cave during the previous exercise, modify the cave for the next drill. Dig out the entryway so that it is larger and has less of a slope. Gradually, the dog needs to become comfortable and familiar with deep, dark places.

Repeat this exercise with the helper as the subject. After the dog is fully competent with this step, set up a drill where the subject does not run away from the dog. Rather, have the dog out of sight as the subject enters the hole. The subject should approach the cave from the upwind side so that the dog will not have a trail to follow. The point is to teach the dog to airscent—nose up to avalanche subjects, not trail—nose down. If the dog has any difficulty understanding this transition from runaway problems, the handler can assist it or the subject can call it.

Step 5: Shallow, Full Body Cave with Blocks

There is little difference between this step and the previous one. Again, begin with runaways and the master as subject. Once the subject is in place, the shoveler places blocks of snow across the entrance to the cave. Begin with soft chunks of snow to facilitate the dog's digging through. The handler can assist the dog while it digs. If the dog is reluctant to dig, the subject can encourage the dog with words or tease it with a reward, sticking it out through the blocks and then pulling it back in. During these early training sessions, you should make a point of taking advantage of the dog's instinctive play and prey drives.

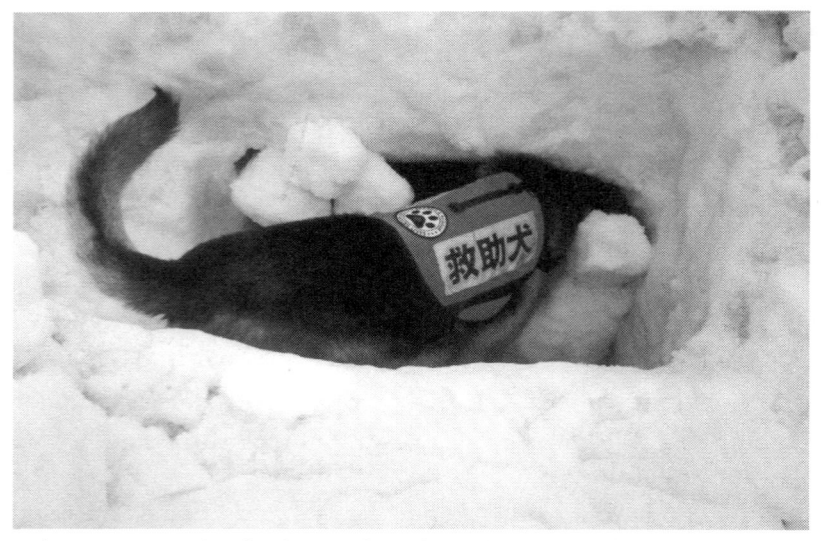

Audi, Japanese avalanche dog, working through a barrier of snow blocks, By Emiko Masuda

Once the dog has successfully found both the master and the helper with and without runaways, move toward installing more blocks of snow with harder consistency. Your goal is to establish progressively more and more barriers between your dog and the subject.

Shovelers covering the blocks with loose snow, By Cullen Lyle

Step 6: Shallow, Full Cave with Blocks and Loose Snow

It is fine to reuse caves, but expect them to settle out with time, making the caves less and less spacious. At this point, your dog should have little difficulty in locating subjects in new caves.

Say goodbye to runaways, but continue using the master as the first subject. With the dog out of sight, place blocks across the entrance and a dusting of loose snow over the blocks. Up to this juncture, we have not incorporated a waiting period. With more snow now, allow about five minutes for the scent to diffuse through the small amount of snow that covers the subject.

During each successive exercise in this step, shovel more and more snow into the hole. Eventually, the loose snow should be up to the top of the hole, flush with the surrounding snow. Take care not to progress too rapidly during this phase. As more snow is incorporated, allow more time for the human scent to rise to the surface. If at any time, the dog has difficulty locating the subject, take a piece of bamboo or a probe pole with a soft end and carefully and slowly probe down through the loose snow into the cave. Make sure to warn the subject that you are doing so and to be prepared to ward off any errant strikes. Do not probe through the roof of the cave—ever.

Step 7: Deeper, Full Cave

Dig a deeper hole, providing three feet of snow over the top of the cave. If the dog is tentative about proceeding into the deeper cave, again provide a ramp. Start with just blocks, and progressively add more loose snow until the hole is flush with the surrounding snow.

Eventually move toward providing four feet of snow over the roof of the cave. This is probably the deepest you will need to construct any of the future caves. We may reuse a cave that has additional snow accumulation on top, increasing the depth; but we try not to use caves that are more than six to eight feet deep.

When the dog consistently finds its master and the helper in deep, full burials, progress to using other people as subjects. Start with the dog's acquaintances and eventually use strangers.

Blind Drills

Your drills for the last few weeks have been full burial caves, not visibly detectable on the surface of the snow. However, the handler knew the locations of the caves and could help the dog if the need arose. Now is the time to incorporate blind problems. These caves have to be dug by someone other than the handler, since the handler should not know the location of the cave. This is a difficult transition for many handlers who, until now, have not had to trust their dogs.

If the dog seriously flounders during the initial blind drills, the shoveler may need to assist by digging down a little ways or by probing through the loose snow, not the roof of the cave. The main point is to instill confidence in the handler that the dog can indeed find people, with no direction from the handler at all.

Multiple Subjects

As dogs become more skilled at the avalanche search game, it becomes a challenge for the handlers to stump their dogs. It may seem as though no matter what you try, your dog aces the drills. Now is a good time to start digging multiple holes in a training area.

Since many avalanche dog's missions and certification tests have multiple subjects, multiple subject drills are more than just a good idea; they are essential. The challenge is the added manpower and time requirements.

Initially place the caves in such a way that the dog will not receive the scent from both subjects at the same time. It is still premature to ask your dog to discriminate the blended scents of two buried people. The caves should not be in line with the wind, but rather across from each other. Make sure that both subjects have rewards. Introduce the concept of finding more than one person gradually by starting with open caves—with no blocks or loose snow blocking the entrance. With each successful find by the dog, place more snow across the entrance, advancing toward full burials.

As the dog searches for multiple subjects, it will alert on the first subject. Allow the dog to dig all the way down to that person and receive its reward. Have the first subject removed from the hole and leave the area, reducing confusion for the dog. Hide the first reward so that the dog understands that the first segment of its problem is completed. Now restart the dog, treating this search the same as the earlier one. Essentially, the dog is doing two separate searches, one immediately following the other.

With success, confidence, and experience in finding two people, you will be able to integrate the multiple subjects into more training scenarios. The key is to work gradually toward the point where your dog is consecutively finding two or more people.

When your dog alerts on the first person, mark the area with a wand. Call for a shoveler to remove about a foot of snow—that person is not to dig all the way down to the first subject. While the first shoveler is digging, begin working the dog again, searching for the second subject. The idea is to teach the dog that it does not need to get instant gratification; the dog can continue working to find more people, which it interprets as more rewards. When the dog locates the second subject, another shoveler digs down about a foot.

At this point, take the dog back to the first alert and see what it does. The dog may alert and dig in the exact place you previously marked. If that is the case, allow it to dig all the way down to the subject to get its reward. Again, remove the reward from the dog's sight so that it understands that that portion of the search is completed. On the other hand, the dog may decide that the scent is stronger in another place, in which case the shoveler again digs down a foot. Return to the second alert to find out what your dog does at that location.

If during any of these steps, the dog returns to an earlier cave that is empty, do not discipline it; just pull the dog away from that location. Direct the dog with your voice, hand signals, or the direction of your walk as to where you would like it to search.

> While multiple subjects can be a logistical nightmare, they can also be a source of great enjoyment and motivation for the dogs. They think they have hit the avalanche dog jackpot.

Multiple Dogs

If done properly, competition between avalanche dogs can be a good thing, especially if a dog has a hard time getting excited about the game. Every now and then, if Sandy was complacent, or even confused, about digging, I brought Hasty in to "up the ante." A little friendly rivalry was all we needed to light a fire under him.

Do not allow dominant dogs to bowl over dogs that are more submissive. A more assertive dog's handler may have to hold the dog off so that the other dog can get its find and reward.

This step demonstrates better than any other step, the importance of mutual respect and cooperation in the presence of subjects and other dogs. If a dog has not learned to share subjects, there may be a need for some behavior modification. It is common at real avalanche missions, to bring another dog over to confirm the alert of one dog. Dogs that cannot tolerate the existence of another dog near their "find" are difficult to control during missions. It is better to discover this weakness during training, not during the real thing.

Multiple Subjects and Dogs

The logistics become even more complicated when you throw multiple dogs and multiple subjects into the formula. When manpower and timing allow it, the result is well worth the effort.

Long Searches

It is common for an experienced dog to uncover a full burial, or even a double burial, in only a few minutes. A dog may go months and never work a training drill longer than 10 or 15 minutes. This is a problem, since most avalanche missions last longer than 10 or 15 minutes. A dog trained to work for a limited amount of time often shuts down after not locating the subject in the normal allotted time.

> It is crucial that handlers realize that a successful search does not always culminate in a find. Success may mean clearing an area so that Mission Base knows that no one is buried there. Your dog must understand that you are pleased with its work even if the dog has not located anyone. The dog's effort alone is worthy of praise.

The way to get around this dilemma is to set up drills where the dog searches an area devoid of subjects for varying lengths of time. This area is adjacent and upwind to the training site. For older, more experienced dogs, increase the desired search time by increasing the size of the area. This teaches dogs that they will not always solve the mystery in a matter of minutes. It also teaches the dog that there will be times when there is no one buried; its assignment is simply to clear an area. We commonly respond to un-witnessed avalanches that appear to have tracks into the slide, and none going out. We can never be certain that someone is not buried there unless we search it.

When we train for longer searches, we typically have someone wait to bury a person in the training area until we are satisfied that the dog has had enough "unsolved mystery" work. Handlers have a tendency to talk to their dogs more often during the longer drills. They worry and nag, telling the dog to search and to get to work. Try to put yourself in your dog's paws. If you are doing your job and someone repeatedly tells you to get to work, don't you start questioning whether you are doing the right thing? Unless your dog is confused, leave it alone and let it do its job. At some point, direct your dog to the area where the subject is buried. Let the dog find, and give it a reward…finally. The celebration after a longer search should reflect your exceeding pleasure with the dog's maturity and perseverance.

As a novice dog handler, I attended an Avalanche School in another county that included such topics as snowpit analysis, stability evaluation, control work, and rescue dogs. I brought my young dog, Hasty, just in case we might have an opportunity to train with another handler. I learned two major lessons that have helped improve my training methods.

First, never train in a vacuum. I do not think that the man who demonstrated the dog portion of the field session had ever watched another avalanche dog work. He dug holes that were not deep enough to be stable. Afraid that they might collapse, he dug them so shallow that a person would not suffocate if they did. He also did not have enough radios; so, he gave the subject a wooden dowel to stick out of the top of the cave if he wanted to get out.

The second lesson I learned was…always, always, always, train more often with real, live subjects than with dummies or articles. This man rarely buried people for his dogs. Consequently, they were not very effective in locating real people.

They were good at finding articles and dummies—that was how they trained. To their credit, they had successfully found a few dead bodies during actual missions. The ironic part was that when I buried the master for his dog, the dog had no motivation to find him. It hit me like a lead balloon that on a real mission, there was a good chance that this dog would bypass a live person to find the dead one. Worse still, she might wait until the victim died to find him.

Article Searches

After a dog becomes adept at locating completely buried people, begin working with articles. Have another person take the article in a clean zip lock bag on to the snow on skis, to eliminate footprints. For early drills, have the person dig a shallow hole, about six inches deep, with a shovel. The person then drops the article from the bag into the hole, reburying it with the shovel. Allow at least 15 to 30 minutes for the scent to rise to the surface. For these initial drills, the handler should know exactly where the article is located so that the dog does not become frustrated.

> Never bury food intentionally for a dog to find. Most of our dogs need little help finding food. Plenty of people on avalanche searches show poor SAR etiquette, leaving food, wrappers, and refuse scattered over the deposition.

Work the dog across the designated area, using a fine grid. Since the article does not contain as much scent as a live body, the dog's nose will have to be closer to the article to detect it. Use a different command than for a live body. I use "Slow Search" and I say it slowly as I start my dogs working. While it is important to reward a dog for an article find, reserve the most intense praise for live finds.

Avalanche dog, Eddy, being rewarded with a backpack that he located, By Patti Burnett

Mock Searches

Mock searches take more manpower, time, creativity, and effort but they are well worth it—for the rescue group or ski patrol as well as the dog. Handlers become frustrated that their training drills are rarely like real avalanches. Such should not be the case for mock drills. I sometimes lie awake at night dreaming up scenarios that we can use. You can have a person digging a hole, yelling to your dog, "check here, check here" in a location far from where the subject is actually buried. Have snowmobiles or snowcats operating in an area upwind of the debris area.

I was asked to do a demonstration for another ski area that did not have a dog program. The Flight for Life helicopter picked Sandy and me up at Patrol Headquarters at Copper Mountain and flew us to the other area. When we arrived, I found a large mound of snow that had been fabricated by snowcats. There were a few snowmobiles overturned in the debris, leaking gas, as well as fumes into the snow and air. People, ski patrollers and guests, covered the debris, and there were another four subjects buried. I was overwhelmed at first, thinking "how unrealistic." But then I considered "No two avalanches that we have been to have been the same, so what's my problem?" As it turned out, Sandy had no trouble, once he figured out the game and I got on the same page. That day helped to solidify in my mind and heart that I could trust my dog.

Cadaver Materials

Those who have spent much time around SAR dog people may have the pleasure of being privy to conversations regarding cadaver materials—real and chemically produced. There are individuals, especially within law enforcement, who spend a great deal of time and effort training their dogs to find victims of crime, disaster, drowning, and exposure. Since it is hard to find subjects for these specific drills—very small joke—it is necessary to replicate the smells as closely as possible. Handlers that specialize in cadaver work may hang around with forensics folks, coroners, or detectives, just hoping that some "material" will fall their way. Some people have all the fun!

Usually by the time rescue dogs arrive at avalanches, most victims have died, either from suffocation or trauma. It makes sense to me that avalanche dog handlers train to find dead victims as well as live. While I believe that articles in some ways replicate the smell of recently deceased victims, should we not also train more purposefully to find those individuals who have been buried for extended periods?

Speaking with experts in the field of cadaver dog work, I learned that the chemically produced scents have subtle differences that we should take into consideration. If using the Sigma Products, Marcia Koenig suggests trying Pseudo-drowned, Pseudo-corpse I, or Pseudo-distressed, since the frozen avalanche victim is not typically as decomposed as other cadaver victims. She says that by burying the material in a tube, it will be more readily retrieved. Another idea is to hide the scent in dummies.

As with other steps in SAR dog training, familiarize the dog initially with the scent on the surface. Then bury the tube shallowly, gradually increasing the depth and size of the search area. It would be interesting to bury a live person and a tube of the chemical separately, to see what the dog does. As Marcia says, "The more situations you train the dog in, the easier it is for the dog to work an actual search." One advantage to using the Pseudo-scent for avalanche training is that it probably has a longer life in the colder temperatures.

SAR dog handlers, who want to avoid the chemicals, may carry zip lock bags with them on avalanche missions, to collect a sampling of the snow that surrounds a deceased victim. Later, they can bury the melted snow with a piece of uncontaminated clothing as a training aid.

> A handler must take certain precautions when using cadaver materials. Learn from the experts how to handle bio-hazardous materials safely.

Whenever possible, try to get your dog to the scene so that it can dig to, or at least smell, a deceased avalanche victim. This is one crucial aspect of training that is not easy to obtain. Even if a dog is not certified, try to bring it to the deposition late in the search to reinforce the dog's aptitude for digging to a dead body. This one event is worth many, many months of training. Arrange for this type of scenario, meeting with the proper authorities, ahead of time. This short window of opportunity occurs before the victim's extrication from the field, while waiting for a coroner or sheriff's officer to investigate, photograph, and document the scene.

6 The Health of Your Avalanche Dog

My Dog
He is my other eyes that can see above the clouds;
My other ears that hear above the winds.
He is the part of me that can reach out into the sea.
He has told me a thousand times over that I am his reason for being.
By the way he rests against my leg.
By the way he wiggles his tail at my smallest smile.
By the way he shows his hurt when I leave without taking him.
(I think it makes him sick with worry
When he is not along to care for me.)
When I am wrong, he is delighted to forgive.
When I am angry, he clowns to make me smile.
When I am happy, he is joy unbounded.
When I am a fool, he ignores it.
When I succeed, he brags.
Without him, I am only just another person.
With him, I am all-powerful.
He has taught me the meaning of devotion.
He is loyalty itself.
With him, I know a secret comfort and a private peace.
He has brought me understanding where before I was ignorant.
His head on my knee can heal my human hurts.
His presence by my side
Is protection against my fears of dark and unknown things.
He has promised to wait for me...whenever...wherever,
In case I need him.
And I expect I will...as I always have.
He is my Dog.
—*Author Unknown*

Function Follows Form—Sandy McFarland

As a breeder of Golden Retrievers, I am extremely conscious of the fact that structure is the most important factor in a good dog's ability to perform. I have had the pleasure of training, showing, and breeding dogs for more than 25 years. I have raised five breed champions who ascended to the top level in obedience, field, and tracking titles. My focus is to produce dogs of correct breed type, with sound minds and bodies. All dogs have OFA hip clearances, ophthalmologist cleared eyes, and hearts cleared by a board-certified cardiologist. To thrive, a dog must have a proper anatomy. A dog should be built in such a way that it performs disciplines without pain or discomfort, without becoming easily fatigued. A structurally sound body will have a lengthy working career.

> "Structure means symmetry of proportion, which provides a smooth, effortless gait, with all parts moving in harmonious rhythm."
> —Rachel Elliott, from her book, *Dog Steps*

The key to good structure is in the balance of the dog's front and rear angles, as well as its overall proportions. It is helpful to study first the skeleton, to recognize correct structure when looking at a coated dog. Underneath all that hair, the skeleton and its surrounding muscles are responsible for the strength and movement of the dog. The purpose of this chapter is to help you visualize correct balance and recognize its importance to the future of a working dog.

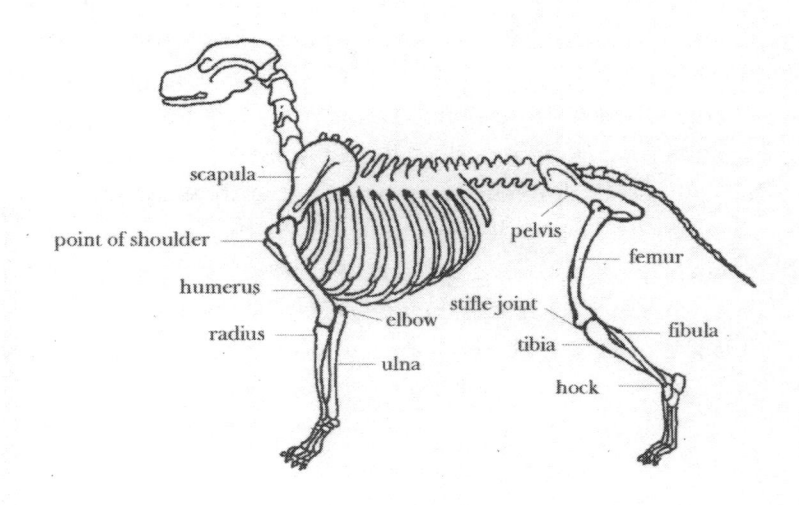

Dog Skeleton, By Sandy Mcfarland

Drawing #1 depicts a dog's basic bone structure, or skeleton. Ligaments that are attached by tendons to the muscles hold the dog's skeleton together. The front assembly includes the sternum (fore-chest) the shoulders, and their attachment at the elbows to the front legs. Below the scapula is the humerus, often referred to as the upper arm. The length of these two bones, their angle of attachment, and the muscles that surround them, are the key to forward motion and the dog's ability to reach out and extend the shoulder, upper arms, and front legs. The ideal shoulder is "well laid back." On the diagram, you can see that there is a 45-degree angle of the shoulder (scapula) to the ground. This is what is meant by correct "shoulder layback."

The hindquarters include the hip joint and its attachment to the upper and lower thigh, the hock, pastern, and the foot. The pelvis should have a 30-degree slant, forming a right angle with the femur at the hip socket. We refer to this area as the hip. The hip joint is comprised of the acetabulum of the pelvis and the head of the femoral bone. The strength of the hip joint is dependent on the depth of the acetabulum and the shape and tightness of the femoral head, which fits into it. Below the femur is the fibula and tibia. These bones need to be long enough to allow the rear leg to extend back with the hock to propel the body forward. Beneath the fibula and tibia is the hock joint which determines the correct direction of the rear feet.

Drawing #2

Drawing #2 depicts a well balanced dog—a dog that has matching front and rear angles.

Chapter 6 The Health of Your Avalanche Dog   83

Drawing #3

Drawing #3 demonstrates a poorly balanced dog that is "upright" or steep in the shoulders and lacking rear angulation. In addition, it has a short second thigh (tibia and fibula.) This poor dog will be short- strided and very stiff after running up and down steep terrain. This dog is not a prudent choice for a working dog.

There is, however, more about the overall structure to consider when selecting a prospective search and rescue dog:

- The ribcage should be deep and well sprung, allowing ample room for a large heart and lung expansion.
- The elbows must fit closely to the ribcage, giving strength to the front assembly.
- The loin should be relatively short, giving strength to a level top-line.
- At a natural stance, all four feet should point forward with no inward or outward twisting of the hocks.
- The feet should be well arched and have thick pads on tight feet. Splayed toes are weak and the gaps between the toes will

become sore as the foot hair collects dirt or huge snowballs on a wintry mountain.

- A moderately long neck will facilitate the dog in stretching its head forward for balance when running up and down mountains.

- Another physical trait that is essential to a working dog is a correct coat. A suitable coat lies close to the body and has a thick under-coat to keep the body warm and a resilient outer-coat to shed snow and water.

> What more could a handler ask for in a search and rescue dog than an animal that is structurally correct, has powerful, well developed muscles and a strong and willing desire to please?

When choosing the future SAR dog from a litter of appealing puppies, keep in mind that a properly balanced seven week old puppy is well-coordinated, even as a baby. Watching the puppy move at a trot tells you if the angles match. The puppy should stand with its front feet well under the body, the rear feet in line with the back of the buttock, all four feet pointing forwards. You should feel for good shoulder layback, depth of body, and tight elbows. These are slightly difficult to recognize in a fluffy puppy, so educate yourself as to what is correct upon palpation. Overall, the puppy should be less "roly-poly" than its littermates and should give the impression of a young athlete. Beware of the tendency to choose the largest puppy in the litter simply because it stands out. A moderately sized youngster will not grow to be heavy or ungainly when it matures.

The following photograph is of AM/Can. CH. Beaumaris Timberee Tessa Ann, UDT.WC. VCX.SHOF. We purchased Tessa from Ann and John Bissette from the Beaumaris Kennel in Conifer, Colorado. Little did I realize that this seven week old blond fluff ball would become one of the top Golden Retrievers of all times. She was a champion at 18 months, and earned titles in all disciplines

Six-week-old puppy, By Sandy Mcfarland

with outstanding scores and multiple highs in trials. Tessa Ann continued her winning ways until the age of 11, when she retired from the show ring to be the "Queen of the House."

Sandy's AM/CAN. CH. Beaumaris Timberee Tessa Ann UDT WC. VCX won Best of Breed at the Eastern and Western Regionals, Best bitch at the National Specialty, and is the only bitch in breed history to win both Best in Show and High in Trial at the same Specialty. Her son, AM/CAN. CH Timberee' Tenacious Token UDT, WCX. VCX, produced breed champions, obedience trial champions, multiple Senior and Master Hunters, the top Agility dog in the country, and is also the sire of Patti Burnett's Sandy.

Best of Show, 1989, National Specialty, By Sandy Mcfarland

What a kick to take Hasty up into Union Bowl during the early season ski packing trips. Snowshoe rabbit style, he hopped through the deep, uncompacted snow. He made all the ski patrollers laugh, creating his own little sloughs, and then riding them out.

Hasty running down steep powder, By Dave Weissman

And, was he every having fun! He was, wasn't he? Well, at least it looked like he was enjoying himself. Now as I think about it, he did get up off his bed slower the next morning. I guess I should have known better than to think he would let me know when it started to hurt. He was doing what I told him to do, just as he always did.

They say that hip dysplasia is one-third genetic, one-third environment, and one-third nutrition. It should have come as no surprise when Hasty's OFA results returned with less than acceptable scores. Who of us would ask our seven-year-old child to run a marathon; and yet that was effectively what I was doing with Hasty. I have had to learn from the mistakes that I made with my first SAR dog. Maybe you and your dog will not have to learn the hard and painful way.

Start Slowly with the Puppies

Despite warnings from more knowledgeable handlers, we all want to take our new SAR puppies out to see what they are made of, just like we would do with new cars. Slow down. Back off. Take a deep breath. Count to ten.

Our young dogs' joints are still developing. Hard surfaces should be avoided whenever possible, especially concrete. I know it hurts my knees and I can only imagine what the impact must feel like to a little puppy.

Hard surfaces are not the only things that are bad for your puppy. Post-holing through steep, uncompacted snow can tear a puppy's ligaments about as quickly as any other type of exercise. The kicker is that steep, uncompacted snow is difficult for avalanche dogs to avoid. It comes with the territory.

At Copper Mountain, we try to select training areas that are close to the duty stations so that the dogs do not have to run as far when they respond to drills. Another reason for training nearby is that the more exposure the dogs have to skiing and snowboarding guests, the more opportunities they have to be injured by ski and snowboard edges.

During patrol sweep, at the end of the day, we used to run the dogs off the hill as we skied down. Unfortunately, the dogs saw it as a race. We got smarter after a while and decided to let the dogs run down the hill only on the flatter snowcat roads. Now, still older and wiser, we hardly ever allow the dogs to run even the flattest roads, and they usually are transported via snowmobiles or toboggans at the end of a workday.

Conditioning & Endurance

Build endurance into your dogs through continuous trotting or swimming. At the ski area, we make it a priority that the majority of our dogs' workouts are uphill, since prolonged downhill running can be harmful, as previously mentioned. The way we have gotten around this challenge is by snowshoeing up the mountain regularly with the dogs. It is good for them, and aerobic exercise can only improve our OWN overall fitness.

Running is my preferred discipline for getting Sandy outside and active, but I have had to learn moderation. When running on asphalt and concrete, I limit the length and intensity of the workout. Concrete is the hardest surface and the absolute worse when it comes to producing impact injuries to humans and canines alike. Ideally, we try to run on dirt and grass trails that are not accessible to vehicles.

SARDOC rescue dog, Gretchen, diving off a river bank, By John Shivek

As a reward for a good run, I usually treat Sandy to a nice cold swim in Lake Dillon. Swimming exercises every muscle and provides a non-weight bearing method of recover after surgery, and various strains and sprains. Some veterinary hospitals even provide hydrotherapy pools for their horses' and dogs' post injury rehabilitation.

I usually cringe when I see people mountain biking with their dogs, off lead or on lead. The dogs have to run downhill at high rates of speed, to try to keep up with the bikes. Any veterinarian will attest that these dogs often experience dehydration and bloody worn-down pads at the least.

If you cross-country ski with your dog, find snow that is well compacted in order to avoid post-holing. Train your dog to avoid ski and snow board edges. We initially travel with our pups, using cross-country skis that do not have metal edges. When the dogs get too close, we tell them to move. If we accidentally hit them, it hurts enough to teach them to stay away, but does not cut their legs or feet. We never allow people on skis or snowboards to play with the dogs.

> "If your dog is fat, you aren't getting enough exercise."
> —Author Unknown

Certain builds of dogs have better stamina. In my experience, medium to smaller boned dogs have greater endurance and are less prone to injury than the larger boned groups. If you allow your SAR dog to gain too much weight, it will be far less fit. Remember that our dogs are athletes and the type and amount of food and exercise we supply them directly affects their performance.

> "Fat does not contribute to performance. In addition to adding dead weight, it places a strain on the cardiovascular system, since every pound of fat contains a mile of capillaries."
> —From *Peak Performance: Coaching the Canine Athlete*, p. 74, by M. Christine Zink, D.V.M., Ph.D.

Agility

Obstacle courses and jumping on and off chairlifts are activities that should wait until the younger SAR dog matures physically. Now is the time to work on building trust and control into your dog. Since agility and dexterity is important for any rescue dog, gradually and sensibly, work up to obstacle work. The effort will pay off when your canine has to work its way through large slabs of avalanche debris.

> Because of previous socialization and obstacle training, when Sandy executed one of his first true agility courses, he was able to complete it confidently, with a high degree of control. A well-socialized rescue dog has a strong foundation for approaching a multitude of scenarios.

Agility Dog, By Purina Incredible Dog Challenge, Carson International

While none of my experience has included the standard agility trials competition, I would strongly recommend it to those unable to do other forms of SAR training during the summer and fall seasons. This would be an excellent way to maintain a rescue dog's sharp mind and body. Please realize that agility equipment can be dangerous, especially for inexperienced puppies. Join a group of accomplished agility teams and get the proper introduction and instructions to obstacles. There are fun matches that you can enter, to help get you and your dog's paws wet, before diving in to full-blown competitions.

According to Holly Newman (www.speakeasy.org/~hnewman/agility) two excellent organizations that host agility competition are North American Dog Agility Council and United States Dog Agility Association. She also recommends Dogwise (www.dogwise.com) and Sitstay (www.sitstay.com) as excellent resources for agility training.

Hydration

I find it harder to water my dogs during avalanche searches than while performing warm environment searches. At the same time, a dog eating snow during an avalanche mission is a common sight. The problem is that eating snow does little, if anything, to hydrate an animal. Rescue dogs become so caught up with the excitement and momentum of the mission, they do not want to drink; and usually the best source of hydration, cold water, does not appeal to their cold bodies, especially mouths.

> Perhaps one of the entrepreneurial handlers in the SAR community could invent a camelback that includes an auxiliary hose for the dogs.

If our rescue dogs refuse H_2O, different ways to get them to drink are to add tomato pastes, or small quantities of powdered flavoring like Kool-aid, Gatorade, or soup mixes to their water. Another trick is to drop a few treats into their water bowls. When the dog submerges its nose to get the treats, the desire to drink kicks in to gear. I have recently learned of a new product on the market called Rebound, intended to re-hydrate active dogs and replenish vitamins and minerals for sick dogs. Other products, specifically designed for hydrating dogs, are constantly popping up on the market.

> "Environmental scientists call dogs and humans "Homeotherms" because they can maintain constant body temperatures, even in the face of extreme outside temperatures. In dogs, the panting center, which stimulates panting, helps the animal get rid of heat. Panting involves rapid shallow breathing that causes evaporation of fluid on the tongue. Dogs have a rich blood supply in their tongues. Heat produced in the dog's muscles and tissues enters the blood and is transported to the tongue, where it is eliminated by panting. Water is important for temperature control because it can hold a lot of heat; it can also carry heat to the surface via the blood steam."
> —Thomas D. Fahey, Ed. D., Exercise Physiology Laboratory
>   California State University, Chico

There are conflicting opinions on the benefits of electrolyte replacement drinks for dogs. Unlike humans, dogs do not regulate their body temperature by sweating; and sweating is generally what causes humans to lose electrolytes. Most veterinary studies have concluded that the advantages of electrolyte replacement drinks are negligible, but not harmful. However, if a dog consumes enough water, it dilutes the existing electrolytes in its system and throws it off balance. In this scenario, an electrolyte replacement drink might be profitable. The objective is to keep your dog hydrated any way possible. If an electrolyte replacement tastes good, it will certainly be more desirable to a dog.

When your dog is well hydrated:
- There is less lactic acid build up in the muscles.
- The dog is better able to regulate its body temperature.
- The nose works far more effectively.

Resting Your Dog During Missions

It is your responsibility, as a dog handler to make sure that your dog gets regular breaks during missions. If it were up to our dogs, they would continue searching all day and night with little rest. Speaking with people who have done long through-hikes with their dogs, the dogs may need more rest than humans—they just will not admit it. Keep in mind that well-trained avalanche dogs will cover perhaps five to ten times the territory at a faster pace than their human counterparts.

Our dogs' motivation may surpass their fitness levels. They need someone else to insist that they stop

Sandy getting his Denver suburb fix to help him apreciate how the other half live, By Rachel Burnett

or slow down, in the same way children need to be told to take naps. At first, this may mean tying them to instill a forced rest. After a while they learn to recognize that when you rest, they rest. The younger the dog and the more stressful the mission, the greater need for frequent and sustained breaks. As a dog gains experience, it learns to pace itself and consequently needs fewer breaks. As a rule of thumb, I try to rest my dogs for about five to ten minutes every hour. Dick Epley was fond of using these breaks for strategy sessions. We get moving so fast and frantically during avalanches that we fail to use our brains as effectively as we could.

> Caroline Hebard rests her dogs ten minutes for every twenty minutes of disaster work. Intense work requires intentional recuperation.

The Value of Your Veterinarian

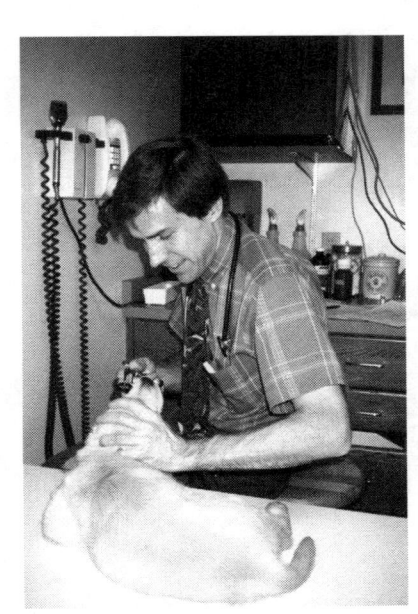

Dr. Tom Fatora examining puppy Sandy, By Patti Burnett

Until your veterinarian has saved your dog's life, you cannot fully appreciate the worth of this individual. Your canine's doctor knows your dog well enough to recognize even the seemingly insignificant nuances of illness or injury

The fall of 2000, I had Sandy at the Animal Hospital of the High Country for a routine visit and Dr. Paul Veralli, our regular veterinarian, had the day off. As an associate checked Sandy out, Dr. Veralli just happened to walk into the examination room. He recognized a slight swelling on Sandy's lip—I thought it was a contusion that was the result of running through the trees during a night search the previous week.

The clinic sent a specimen to a pathologist at Colorado State University, who confirmed Dr. Veralli's suspicions; Sandy had a Grade II Mast Cell Tumor, a very aggressive form of cancer, especially in the highly-vascular mouth. Sandy had a portion of his lip and maxilla surgically removed, as well as a canine tooth; and they were able to get completely clean borders around the excision. There was no need for chemotherapy or radiation. I hate to think of what might have happened had Dr. Veralli not recognized the abnormality. Your veterinarian should be your canine's and your best friend.

Dr. Rob Hilsenroth, Executive Director of Morris Animal Foundation, presenting award to Sandy and Patti at 2002 meeting at Keystone, By Morris Animal Foundation

7 Scent and Snow

Brad and Todd chose an autumn day in November 1992 to ice-climb a glacier on the northwest flank of Flattop Mountain in Rocky Mountain National Park. Brad, an instructor with the Colorado Mountain School in Estes Park, was giving Todd some technical ice-climbing pointers. Over the course of the day, as is common in the Colorado Rockies, a fast moving front developed, accompanied by strong winds and heavy snow accumulations. At the top of the glacier, a dangerous cornice dangled high above the men, growing larger, minute by minute.

Suddenly, with no warning, the cornice broke free and an early season avalanche swept both men off the ice, burying them deeply. Two friends who witnessed the event, remembered seeing a "whoosh of air and then a glove zooming by." Because of constant avalanche danger in the months following the accident, a rescue was not attempted until the following summer.

On August 9, Search and Rescue Dogs of Colorado deployed three avalanche dog teams, along with support personnel. The Park Service provided helicopter service to facilitate transportation needs. I was struck by the irony of searching for men buried under ice and snow in 70 and 80-degree temperatures. Equipped with crampons and ice axes, we slowly and deliberately worked a search pattern up and down the steep glacier.

The dogs' most animated alerts began close to one of the rock formations on the outer curve of the slide path. From that point, we marked alerts that descended vertically all the way to the glacier pool at the bottom. Hasty and Doc, an Aspen dog certified in avalanche, water, and wilderness air scent, were both notably agitated around the edge of the water and gave alerts consistent with a submerged body.

Unfortunately, because the snow was as much as 17 feet deep, and the ice layers inpenetrable, we were unable to locate either of the men at that time. A year later after a prolonged thaw, Rocky Mountain National Park rangers located the men's remains in an area congruent with the dogs' alerts. My speculation is that the men's bodies were lodged between two layers of ice. Melting ice and snow flowed over the victims onto one of the ice layers. As the water passed the bodies, it accumulated scent and carried it to the glacier pond at the bottom of the snowfield.

Why Do Dogs Smell So Good?

I can tell you for a fact that my dog, Sandy, does not always smell so good. But, most of the time, I wonder what it is about his nose that makes him smell so well.

> **Do not lose the amazing significance of a dog's ability to smell a human, trapped under tons of snow.**

With dog noses, bigger is nearly always better. The vomeronasal organ is located in the roof of a dog's mouth. Its function is to collect and classify scent, in much the same way that the receptors in the nose folds do.

> **Caroline Hebard states in her book, So That Others May Live, that one-eighth of a dog's brain is dedicated to the sense of smelling. She goes on to say that humans have 5 million smell receptor cells. Dogs have 220 million!**

It is believed that dogs are able to detect some scents that are in concentrations as modest as one part per trillion. A dog's nose operates so actively that you can audibly hear it working. You may even see a dog's mouth taste, or lick, the scent. Some dogs have better noses and those dogs usually have a greater desire to use their noses. Training aids a dog's scent ability as the dog learns that successful scenting produces big dividends. We may never understand exactly what it is about those muzzles. However, what we do know is that we should make it our business to best position search and rescue dogs so that their noses can be used to the greatest advantage.

> **Teaching a puppy to use its nose is great fun because the sense of smell is more developed than the sense of sight. During dry land runaway games, I marveled at how Hasty would follow ground scent so intently that he would actually run headfirst into his subject. Was he ever surprised!**

What Does Scent Do In Snow?

The human body is constantly sloughing dead cells. According to Jan and Bill Syrotuck, a person sheds 40,000 dead cell rafts every second, (taken from Caroline Hebard's book.) When scent particles slough off a buried body, they are picked up by air vapors rising to the snow's surface. The vapors ascend through the snow faster the greater the difference between the ground and the snow surface temperatures. Snow scientists call this phenomenon temperature gradient. The ground temperature is nearly always warmer than that of the snow surface, and the warmer air molecules rise.

The scent follows the path of least resistance. Frequently, this trajectory is not directly above the buried person. Many contingencies redirect scent. In a hard slab avalanche with large chunks of snow, the scent escapes more effectively around the chunks than through them. If there are trees in the deposition area, the scent may rise through the tree-wells and branches, which typically offer more air space. As sited in the story about the glacier search, ice layers also cause a deviation of scent.

Japanese SAR dog, Audi, looking for scent, By Emiko Masuda

Is It Ever Too Cold To Search?

In my experience, it has never been too cold. In fact, when it comes to avalanche dog search work, the chillier the better. When the air is colder, the scent diffuses through the snowpack more rapidly because of the larger temperature gradient. In fact, I believe it to be true that dogs have greater difficulty locating scent during warm weather searches. The theory is that an inversion layer traps the scent on the surface of the snow. Consequently, the wind does not pick it up to create a scent cone. In similar scenarios, a good strategy is to work a closer, finer search grid.

> Training during storms and colder temperatures directly affects the performance of our dogs during actual avalanche call-outs. Fair weather trainers can expect their dogs to be fair weather performers.

When people assert that it is too cold to search, their rationalization may be more a factor of comfort than ideal search conditions. Realize that I live in Colorado where the cold air is dryer and probably more moderate than in the Pacific Northwest. Fellow SAR dog handlers from Montana and Alaska tell me that their dogs have no problem searching in minus 30-degree temperatures. Dog handlers learn to cope with the radical environments where they live and work. Extreme weather is a catalyst for extreme avalanches. Colorado does occasionally have temperatures that drop into the minus 20's, but that is more the exception than the rule.

> The dogs often fare better than their human counterparts during exceptionally cold searches.

For those interested in scientific evidence, Jane and John Aspnes did a two-year study in Fairbanks, Alaska in the mid-1990s with buried material. Natives of the Northern Country know a thing or two about cold. They gave an outstanding presentation of their findings at the NASAR Conference in 1998. Their conclusion was that cold did not affect the dog's scent abilities.

What about the Wind?

Another factor that affects scent transport is the wind velocity and direction. The stronger the wind, the greater the likelihood that the dog will alert downwind of the burial site. Count on it. Because air is constantly moving through the snowpack, the wind even affects scent below the snow surface.

Extremely gusty, strong winds are more difficult for dogs to work then steady, moderate winds. The winds can disperse the scent so rapidly that the dogs may have difficulty finding a manageable scent cone. Again, the best strategy is to slow the dog down, working a smaller grid pattern.

> As Roger Caras has remarked, "A dog's nose is something for us to wonder at. It is perfectly remarkable and reminds us that there is a world out there that we can never know. At least not as human beings."
>
> —By Masson, taken from *Dogs Never Lie About Love*, page 199.

Length of Burial Time

We have had experience searching for people buried for as short as 14 minutes and as long as a year. If you are fortunate enough to arrive on scene early, scent may not have had sufficient time to rise to the surface. Be patient and allow your dog to do its magic. Do not turn down a search request, thinking that a body has been buried for too short or too long.

> "The diffusion rate can run between one minute per meter or less in Colorado powder to 15 minutes per meter in Pacific wet cement. A good average for the experienced dog is two minutes per meter. For the novice dog, wait longer than your longest estimate to give him a continuous column of scent through the pack that he can scent down to the buried person."
>
> —By Sandy Bryson in her book *Search Dog Training*

Dogs have successfully found people who have been buried for extended periods. For longer burials, depending upon the temperature and depth, the body may be either quite decomposed or well preserved. Obviously, there is more scent with the decomposed bodies; and cadaver dogs, have an easier time locating them.

> "Because scent always has been part of the canine skills, training dogs in those activities involving scent actually means teaching them to apply on command an inborn ability to search out or follow a designated scent."
> —By Pearsall and Dr. Verbruggen, from *Scent, Training to Track, Search, and Rescue*, page xii

Roxanne, Crested Butte Patrol dog—a study in focus. By Jack Gibbons

8 Certification

Good News

Certification is more than just a good idea. This instrument is employed in all aspects of SAR dog work to provide goals for developing teams, as well as evaluation standards. Without clearly defined standards, there is no way for a team to know whether it is adequately prepared to respond to missions!

Certification is also important for the unlikely event of having to defend one's training records and achievements.

In avalanche search dog work, it usually only takes one or two winter seasons for a team to achieve operational status. More typically, wilderness airscent and trailing certification takes two or more years of consistent training and experience.

Bad News

The bad news is that the certification process can take on a life of its own. Handlers become so obsessed with passing the almighty test, that they lose sight of the ultimate goal. When it comes time to respond to missions, they need to be the best avalanche dog team they can be. At that point, how well they did impressing the testers pales in significance. Unfortunately, to get to that point we all have to jump through certain hoops, crossing all the T's and dotting all of I's.

Search and Rescue Dogs of Colorado Avalanche Certification Test*

*as taken from the SARDOC Standards

Search and Rescue Dogs of Colorado certifies a few avalanche dogs each year. The dogs must be at least a year old. Non-ski patrol dogs must first wilderness certify in either air scent or trailing before attempting certification in any of the special disciplines; i.e., cadaver, water, avalanche, and evidence. Handlers acquire letters of confidence from fellow SAR dog handlers, ski patrollers, and rescue group members indicating that the signed individuals have witnessed their competence, consistency, and commitment.

Qualifications

The simulated avalanche area is at least 150 feet top to bottom and 100 feet across. It is preferable to dig the caves a day or two in advance, in at least six feet of snow, having a minimum of three feet of snow above the ceiling of the cave. The area should be completely disturbed with shovels to simulate avalanche debris and to distribute distracting scent. The subjects should be people who are not familiar to the dog. They are buried out of sight from the test team, while a backpack, not having the scent of anyone in the test area, is also buried a few feet deep.

The handler and dog must approach and navigate rapidly and carefully, despite radio interruptions and persons on the perimeter. The handler is given a witness account by the reporting party and instructed to commence. When the dog indicates the first subject, it is diverted and restarted, while a shoveler digs a shallow hole. When the dog indicates the second subject, it is again diverted and returned to the first hole to test for a re-indication. If the dog digs accurately and positively, it is permitted to fully recover that subject and receive its reward. The dog must locate both live subjects within 30 minutes. The dog need not locate the backpack. Indications on the backpack will be handled like a live subject, and the team will continue searching for the actual live subjects. The testers will then observe the enthusiasm differential in the dog's indications for the backpack versus the live subjects.

Testing Rules for Avalanche Search

- Nothing belonging to the handler is permitted in the cave with the subject.
- Only inaudible beacons are used.
- Subjects, testers, and shovelers enter the slide zone from the windward side or from a different direction than the test team will enter.
- Shovelers and testers are positioned in a way that does not cue the dog or handler.
- Entire slide area is disturbed. As you can see, avalanche tests are not entered into lightly; many man-hours go into holding a good test.
- After the area disturbance, the test should run as soon as possible, allowing at least 15 minutes for percolation of scent.
- All caves must have a minimum of three feet of snow on top of them.
- Full body caves are preferred; the cave must be a minimum of a head and shoulder cave.
- The subject must have a working radio and beacon.

Handler Considerations

- The handler must have completed an acceptable avalanche course and be able to demonstrate a working knowledge of avalanche safety.
- The handler must successfully complete a written or oral avalanche exam.
- The handler must agree to have an avalanche beacon and shovel when responding to missions.

- The handler must be capable of selecting and inhabiting an adequate campsite for the team, for a minimum of 24 hours, during any weather conditions encountered by the team above timberline and in deep snow.
- The handler must be competent in winter travel.

Dog Considerations

- The dog must have a suitable natural coat and stamina to withstand and work effectively in below zero temperatures and navigate avalanche debris.
- Any dog showing signs of unstable and/or undesirable behavior under normal conditions will not be certified.

Training Requirements

- Dog and handler teams are encouraged to work regularly on their own on all phases of training.
- Training recommended is two to three times a week.
- The handler must participate in at least two of the four SARDOC formal training sessions each year.
- The handler must complete an avalanche course every three years.

Required Equipment

In addition to the supplies necessary for every SAR dog handler, the following equipment is also required for avalanche search.
- Cross-country skis, mountaineering equipment, or snowshoes
- Back-packable avalanche shovel
- Rescue beacon

There are three evaluators; two help prep the area and one has no knowledge of, is blind to, the locations of the caves. Once the site has been prepped, subjects have been buried, and testers, shovelers, and observers are off the "debris" for at least 15 minutes,

Japanese mountain rescue team probing Audi's Alert, By Emiko Masudo

the test begins. The dog team and "blind" evaluator are brought to the test site and briefed that at least two people have been buried in this location. The test team has 30 minutes to locate both victims. The testing handler advises the evaluators of strategy and any subsequent changes in tactics as they occur. The two evaluators, who know where the victims are located, remain on the edges of the slide path.

As the dog gives alerts, the handler communicates with the blind evaluator, who remains with the testing team while they work. With the first alert, the handler flags the area and calls for a shoveler. The shoveler digs down about one-foot in the area the handler directs him. The shoveler then returns to the edge of the debris. Meanwhile, the handler instructs the dog to continue working to find any remaining subjects. When the next alert occurs, the other shoveler receives similar instructions to those of the first shoveler. The handler then has the dog return to the first flagged area with hopes that the dog will re-alert in that location and dig down to the subject, whereupon he is rewarded. The same occurs with the second subject.

Scores are given for such things as:

- handler strategy
- dog alerts
- dog enthusiasm
- handler's preparation and competence in backcountry travel
- handler's knowledge of avalanche control, safe routes, evaluation, and rescue
- handler's reading of dog
- endurance of dog
- handler's judgment of sweep of the area
- handler's ability to give probability of detection

Extreme self-confidence... *Source unknown.*

Summit County Avalanche Deployment Dog Test

The test used to evaluate Summit County ski patrol teams that are not member of SARDOC is slightly different from the previously mentioned test. Teams search an area that is 100' x 100' and have 20 minutes to locate both subjects. Of the three evaluators, at least one or two of them have to belong to an organization other than that of the testing team. We implemented this test to satisfy Flight for Life's requirement that all dogs that fly with them have an avalanche certification.

Cramming for the Test

Sometimes our dogs' memories get them into trouble when testing time rolls around. Take care that, in the weeks preceding a test, you do not train in the area where the test is scheduled. A number of years ago, I did a practice drill with our second rescue dog, Sandy, right before his avalanche test. On the day of the test, despite the fact that the old holes were completely filled in, he initially went to those locations.

Run mostly double, blind drills where the handler does not know the locations of the two caves. If the dog has problems, continue doing blind doubles, but make them shallower and have a shoveler nearby who knows exactly where the subjects are buried. Work on enthusiasm and speed. If the testing team lacks enthusiasm, bring in other dogs with which the testing dog can compete.

Most of all, relax and good luck. If you are nervous, your dog will be the first to notice. As long as you are prepared, what is there to worry about? If you fail, you will not be the first ones and you just might learn a valuable lesson. If you pass, the hard work has just begun.

9 Search Strategy

On March 15, 1987, Randy and Steve were highmarking a ridge above Shrine Pass. Around noon, we showed up at the Vail Pass rest area after receiving a report that a large avalanche had buried two brothers and their snowmobiles. The outpouring of support, manpower, food, and equipment, from Copper Mountain was enormous. Snowmobiles transported the three dog teams to the site, and the reporting party, who witnessed the burial of his friends, gave a short briefing. He told us that he was certain that they were in the northern part of the deposition since that was where he watched them disappear into the cloud of snow.

I began working Hasty at the toe of the northern portion of the debris, but his nose kept pulling him over to the south side. Trying to help him out with my 'superior brain power,' I called him back to where I was sure Randy and Steve were buried; but he returned to his original area of interest. I asked myself, "Now who is the leader here?" Five hours later, the young men, and their snowmobiles were located close to the toe under six feet of snow—on the south side, exactly where Hasty had been trying to show me. The force of the avalanche had overturned both machines, their fuel completely drained out of them. There is good reason to allow our canine partners to be the leaders when it comes to technical nose work.

However, this rationalization should not prevent us from developing a good strategic plan for every search.

Any Dog's Better Than No Dog At All...Not

I have heard stories of avalanche accidents where rescuers found the buried person's dog sitting on top of the debris. Lo and behold, the master was buried directly beneath where the dog was sitting. Reports such as this, lead people to assume that any dog is better than no dog on an avalanche search. No conscientious SAR team sends an unqualified person into the field and this should hold true for rescue dogs as well. They become liabilities to the SAR group and may prevent the fielding of more qualified dogs. The greatest risk is that an untrained dog will miss the victim when they have supposedly "cleared" an area.

When avalanche accidents occur, well-intentioned people and dogs come out of thin air. At one of our first large avalanche missions, a man arrived from Canon City, the location of the Colorado State Penitentiary. He had an aggressive hybrid wolf and insisted that his wolf could find people. In no time at all, this man was escorted out of the area. Incidentally, we found his backpack after his departure and it contained a gun. We all wondered whether perhaps he would use the gun on his wolf if he chose to fight with one of our less "manly" dogs.

These days, especially, there are few excuses for sanctioning an untrained dog. Every year there are more and more dogs qualified for avalanche, water, disaster, cadaver, wilderness, and evidence search. I would hate to think that I harmed the credibility and reputation of search and rescue dogs because I persuaded command to work a non-operational dog. Once an agency has witnessed the antics of an untrained dog, it may never deploy dogs again. Too many SAR dog people have spent too much time laying valuable groundwork for us to think only of our size large egos.

Trust Your Dog

Believe your dog and do not let anyone try to convince you otherwise. There are times when my best strategy is no strategy at all. We have had a lot of success when I just let my dogs do their job. They have already proved that they are worthy of my trust.

When I arrive at a mission base, I start by getting all of the pertinent information. A handler needs to know the last seen point, prevailing wind directions, a weather forecast, the number of victims, search resources already deployed, depth of deposition, results of other dog's work, remaining avalanche hazard, etc. However, as soon as we have clearance to go, I often allow my dogs to do a hasty search of the debris, to see if they pick up scent right away. I have the troublesome task of standing back and watching…with my mouth shut.

Keep in mind that patience is a virtue; and the reason you were asked to participate is more about your dog's excellent nose than your superior brain. It is quite common for a dog to catch the scent during the initial sweep of the area and start digging. I am not sure what to attribute this fact to; I just know it works. Some dogs take more readily to this indiscriminate type of searching. Those dogs accustomed to chatty and overly controlling handlers may find the silence intimidating; those who are independent, love having the autonomy to work with no restrictions and interruptions.

If after 10 to 15 minutes, the dog has not been able to hit upon a scent, help the dog out by selecting a grid pattern, working the dog over it thoroughly and systematically. Again, I caution you to let your dog work. Do not interfere any more than necessary.

> *I watched Hasty, normally a happy, enthusiastic dog, crouch down low, tail between his back legs. He slowly approached an area where the victim was likely to have been buried. He dropped his nose to the snow and then ever so subtly scratched the surface with one of his paws. As he scratched a little deeper, I noticed that the tip of his tail, still between his legs, wagged ever so slightly.*

This behavior was new to me, a novice avalanche dog handler. Hasty was telling me that he had found someone who smelled significantly different from the people he normally found.

Hasty had met the scent of death.

Slow Search

In my experience, and that of other handlers, it can be a challenge to recognize a dog's alerts on dead bodies. When first working around cadaver scent, expect your dog to act strangely, exhibiting uncharacteristic behavior. He may roll, urinate, defecate, whine, crouch low, leave, or just sniff slightly—all indications that the person buried smells differently from most of the people he finds during training.

I expressed my frustration to Dick Epley when Hasty was young and still not giving me the kinds of alerts I needed on avalanches.

Dick Epley's beautiful Shepherd patiently waiting, By Dan Burnett

Dick, one of the few great SAR dog handlers, had an uncanny ability to both read dogs and develop search strategy. When he approached an avalanche accident, he would survey the scene and arrive at the most logical strategies, leaving the rest of us scratching our heads, wondering, "How'd he know that?"

Dick taught me a training procedure he called "slow search." He had concluded that the reason our dogs gave such weak alerts on dead bodies was that we normally trained with live subjects, using a "search" command. It made sense that, under the search command, the dogs would not alert as enthusiastically on the dead victims as they had on the live. He suggested that in order to condition our dogs to alert stronger on dead victims, we had to use a different command: slow search. We trained on articles when we were using the slow search command. The dogs quickly learned that they could look for a scent that was different from that of a live person. That scent was more like residual scent or a dead body, and it was acceptable to dig it up.

Now, when we arrive on avalanche searches, we begin working with the "search" command so that if there are victims who are still alive, the dogs will find them first. Usually, I switch to the "slow search" command within 30 to 60 minutes, depending on the elapsed time since burial. I have been pleasantly surprised how much this training has changed the type of alerts my dogs display on missions with dead bodies. The other advantage to this additional command is that now the dogs more readily find clues; i.e., backpacks, skis, poles, etc. These clues may ultimately help in the location of buried victims.

POD/POA

There are times when outsiders to SAR jargon wonder how we come up with this stuff. POA refers to the Probability of Area. We assign higher POAs to places where avalanches are more likely to deposit their victims. Common areas are at the toe of the slide, in a tree well, at the bottom of a cliff, on the outside of a corner, or on a bench. A search boss will typically assign the greatest number of resources to the highest POA sectors.

POD refers to Probability of Detection. If a dog team searches an area and feels 70% confident that the victim is not buried there, they assign the area a 70% POD. Another way of explaining this is that if the person were in the area, there is a 70% chance that the team would have located that person. For an avalanche dog team, the highest PODs require moderate, steady wind, a deposition depth less than 10 feet, dog and handler working well together, and few distractions.

Ultimately, your goal in clearing an avalanche is to report back to mission base, that you have a high degree of certainty that there is no one buried in the area to which you were assigned. When not certain, it is always wise to allocate a lower POD. With a low POD and a high POA, mission base may choose to send additional resources into the area.

Be realistic and recognize the fact that our dogs are not machines. They have as much right to an "off day" as we do. They may not be feeling well. They may not be handling either the hot or the cold temperatures optimally. If a team has had to run all the way to an avalanche site, without mechanical transportation assistance, the dog may be fatigued and unable to perform at the highest level. In such situations, it is your responsibility to assign a lower POD.

Snowmobiles

With powerful machines, able to climb incredibly steep inclines, the entire county is seeing many more cases of buried snowmobilers. Another reason snowmobilers are experiencing greater exposure is that they have built an alliance with snowboarders and skiers to help them get into the steeper and less accessible backcountry terrain. When accidents occur, many of these individuals are buried in close proximity to their machines. It is customary for the snowmobiles to be inverted, their gas emptied into the surrounding snow.

Patti directing Hasty to begin working, By Copper Mountain Resort,

    In my earlier avalanche dog training days, I painstakingly tried to limit Hasty's exposure to helicopter, snowcat, vehicle, and snowmobile fumes. I had heard, and I still believe it to be true, that exposure to fumes can de-sensitive a dog's nose for an undetermined period. I even remembered reading about an avalanche that occurred in New Zealand, in which a rescue helicopter selected a landing zone on the edge of the debris. Rescue dogs were unable to locate the victim until after the helicopter had left—they subsequently located the victim directly under the LZ. Therefore, limiting the dog's exposure to fumes during actual missions is an important consideration.

    However, I now approach training differently. We try to set up sporadic drills where the dogs have to use their noses in the presence of those nasty fumes. This strategy has served us well, for now the dogs do not feel compelled to completely avoid and turn their noses off with the first whiff of fuel-operated equipment. When they come under adverse and diverse conditions, they learn to adjust. Even in gas-saturated snow, an expected contingency when searching for buried snowmobilers, the dogs find their victims.

I still try to avoid fumes when we are on actual missions to increase Sandy's ability to find the victim sooner; but I am not as paranoid about maintaining total avoidance as I used to be.

How Much Do I Blab?

Unfortunately, many people regard avalanche dogs as miracle workers. Turn them on and abracadabra; there is the victim. I used to believe this myth myself. Dog handlers take heed—beware of drawing too much attention to yourself and your dog. Just because you have a radio does not mean you need to use it all the time. When in doubt, keep your mouth shut. There is a tendency for new, inexperienced handlers to announce to everyone out there in radio-land that their dogs have "gotten a hit" and the victim is definitely "right here." What happens when such an announcement is made? Resources are pulled off their current tasks and reassigned to the dogs' areas of interest. Unless you are fairly certain that the interest your dog has is bomb proof, take other steps. Bring other dogs over to verify your dog's curiosity. Probe the area. Remember that until you have gotten a strike, it could be an article, a dead animal, or possibly scent that is escaping to the surface far from the victim's location.

Avalanche Deployment

One of the most exciting innovations I have had the privilege of participating in is Avalanche Deployment. It was apparent to us that European rescue dogs had a track record of finding far more avalanche victims alive than we in the United States; and we were interested in knowing why that was the case. Part of the explanation had to do with the fact that they had many more avalanche burials than we did. However, we were convinced that there had to be other reasons as well.

We discovered that European rescue teams reserve more helicopters and SAR dog teams for the specific task of avalanche search.

Flight for life helicopter, by Dan Burnett

At the first sign of an accident, a team is deployed with an avalanche dog and handler, and often a physician or medic.

At Copper Mountain, we enjoyed an excellent working relationship with our medical helicopter service, Flight for Life. In 1993, a steering committee met to create criteria, objectives, and guidelines for a new program called Avalanche Deployment. That group was comprised of the following representatives:

- Summit County and Alpine Rescue Groups
- Summit and Clear Creek County Sheriff's Offices
- Copper Mountain, Loveland, Arapaho Basin, Keystone and Breckenridge Ski Patrol
- Flight Nurses and Pilots

The Avalanche Deployment team is comprised of a snow safety technician, an avalanche dog, and a dog handler. The dog team has to pass a stringent avalanche dog certification and maintain good standing with its particular SAR or Ski Patrol organization. Each member of the Avalanche Deployment team is responsible for annually watching a helicopter safety video, as well as attending a training session, including at least one hot-load and unload before December 15. They must also subsequently complete monthly helicopter briefings—practicing with doors, seatbelts, radios, and helmets. Avalanche Deployment Team members carry cards that verify compliance with regular training sessions.

If a call is received by either 911 (County Dispatch), or one of the local ski patrols that there has been an avalanche accident, the Sheriff's Office determines whether an Avalanche Deployment should be implemented. If the answer is in the affirmative, the closest, most qualified, team deploys. The designated team responds to the Medical Center's LZ or a designated LZ, often at the summit of one of the ski areas. The snow safety technician is either a SAR group member or ski patroller.

The responding team does a flyby of the reported slide to ascertain whether there has, in fact, been a burial and whether they can safely effect a search in the area. The final decision on the viability of landing the helicopter lies solely with the pilot. If able to land

Julie Kelble, flight nurse, treating an avalanche patient, By Provenant Health Partners

near the avalanche, the team is hot-unloaded and the helicopter leaves to get either more rescue personnel or the flight nurse.

We have effectively implemented this program a number of times in Summit and Clear Creek Counties. The ability to respond in a rapid manner reduces the chances of injuring rescue members and increases the possibility that some day we will find an avalanche victim alive.

Two of the most incredible helicopter pilots and a wonderful flight nurse that we flew with have subsequently died in accidents while performing other important rescue assignments—not avalanche deployment. Before signing on to an avalanche deployment program, decide in your own heart whether you are willing to take the risks necessary to complete your assignments. Helicopters are not toys and deserve a high degree of respect and concern.

Knowing When to Call It Quits

Sometimes SAR is a lot like searching for a needle in a haystack. These missions often involve unwitnessed avalanches. By all outward appearance, tracks enter the deposition, but there are none departing it. The only acceptable choice is to search the debris. The sad part about these scenarios is that they are usually preventable. If people who trigger these avalanches would report them to the local ski patrol or search and rescue group, hundred of man-hours could be avoided. Unfortunately, people are either too ignorant or afraid of reprisal.

The decision to suspend search efforts is always difficult. What if there really is someone in there? How could I live with myself knowing that I had left someone under the snow?

> "Most of the important things in the world have been accomplished by people who have kept on trying when there seemed to be no hope at all."
> —Dale Carnegie

The decision-making is somewhat simplified if there has not been a report of a missing person. However, the resolution to suspend search operations is never an easy one.

When the Risk is Too Great

Disaster and avalanche searches are two areas where it is most critical that SAR personnel be on their toes. A friend recounted to me the story of a response their ski patrollers made to an out-of-bounds accident with a confirmed burial. As searchers arrived, in their haste to find the victim, they triggered another slide, which buried some of the rescuers. Suddenly a search for one avalanche victim became exponentially more extensive and urgent.

Avalanche dog handlers commonly respond to accidents in unfamiliar terrain in the backcountry. I regularly ask myself whether those running the SAR operation have a firm grasp of snow dynamics and avalanche rescue. Will they have the resources to determine whether we can safely enter the field and effect a cautious recovery? I usually try to respond with my own snow safety technician, so that there is some collaboration in making the weighty decisions that accompany avalanche rescue. To my amazement, most mission coordinators welcome input from an outside resource that speaks with humility, experience, and authority.

Never become a liability to the mission command staff. God has given you common sense and a brain to analyze the relative safety of a given scenario. If you have any doubt about entering the field, voice those concerns to the appropriate people.

> You will not help anyone if you become a second casualty in your haste to find an avalanche victim. It is always better to be safe than sorry.

Decades ago, as a new patroller on an avalanche control route, I took a short ride through the trees when an unexpected slide broke loose. Afterwards, one of the less experienced patrollers tongue-lashed the route leader for taking us into that area. He said that he had not felt good about going there in the first place. I remember the route leader responding, "You have no right to tell me that now. If you had expressed your apprehension from the beginning, we would have turned around. Even as a less experienced snow worker, your anxieties are valuable and you will be heard."

> "Familiarization and prolonged exposure without incident, lead to a loss of appreciation of risk."
> —Dr. Ken Kamler, 1996 Everest Expedition Doctor

10 Mission Base

We have Hasty the dog; I really don't need anyone else. After all, how far could a woman with only one leg have wandered from the camp?

Why bring in any more resources in the middle of a snowing night? What's up with those ten officers surrounding the man in handcuffs?

—Dan Burnett

Interagency Relations with the Dog Resource—Dan Burnett

Note: Dan Burnett has been my faithful companion and life partner since 1984 and is the father of our two children, Beth and Rachel. Dan has been a mission coordinator with the Summit County Rescue Group since 1980 and has a vast amount of experience in every aspect of mountain rescue. He practices Real Estate to support our SAR habits.

Dan & Patti On 14,000 Blanca Peak, By Dan Burnett

Are there correct and incorrect ways to view the avalanche dog team? Incident Commanders, who have insufficient experience deploying rescue dogs, need foreknowledge in the proper use of this valuable resource.

Mountain rescue has always been a team effort—which is one of the reasons people enjoy search and rescue work. It turned out that the handcuffed man mentioned earlier was two things—he was the reporting party as well as an escaped convict, wanted and feared by the police. When he refused to meet me, dreading police involvement, I told him, "No meeting—No search." As soon as he agreed to a rendezvous, I sent a couple of officers to precede me.

The simple story was that, upon his escape from prison, he and his wife had gone camping. A fight ensued and she stormed out of the tent, into the drifting snow. "She couldn't have gone far, she only has one leg." What a great story and a dog specific mission, I thought.

Hours into the search, local police officers located her in her Aurora condominium. Rats! My entire strategy had revolved around the use of search dogs close to the campsite; and she showed up 80 miles away.

If you are lucky, no one else will be aware of how dumb a mission coordinator can be. Apparently, God was watching out for me. The Sheriff's officers assigned to find out where she lived did much more. They tracked down her residence and sent an Aurora police officer there. Somehow, she had managed to hike five miles to the main road and then hitchhiked home—leaving a very worried and "soon to be imprisoned" husband.

This mission illustrates one of three kinds of search managers. Some managers like to place all of their eggs in the "dog-is-all-we-need" basket. However, the "leave-the-dog-home-we-don't-need-a-mascot" type of coordinator is just as inappropriate as the latter. Even the "some-of-my-best-friends-are-search-dogs-and-their-handlers" type mindset is not ideal.

There is only one correct attitude for a search manager, coordinator, field team leader, sheriff, ski patrol, etc. A search is a complicated team effort. To be most effective, we have to regard the dog on an equal level with the other available tools. Never rely totally on the dog, helicopter, rescue beacon, radio, the lost person intelligence or profile, snowmobile, probe line, or witness.

Command must work to develop a many-faceted dog program. Use rescue dogs, even when there is only a slight chance of success. Many, many times, one dog can do the work of 40 searchers; and, often, the dog may be the very best resource to solve an unsolvable problem.

> "One rescue dog can search the area of deposition as much as eight times faster than a twenty person probe team. The dog can locate a victim by scent thereby becoming an important tool in any avalanche accident especially an in-area avalanche where the victim may not be carrying a transceiver. A good dog team can save lives, time, and money."
> —From the Crystal Mountain Avalanche Rescue Dog Program and Training Manual, Faith Clark and Elaine Marquez, 1993

On the other hand, it is ignorant to think that dogs can do it all. A dog may be less proficient if exposed to gas fumes or if weather conditions prohibit the optimal use of its nose. However, it is close-minded not to use a dog simply because a mission coordinator does not like dogs. Yes, it does happen. In my opinion, at least one-third of all people secretly detest dogs.

Last, there are search mangers that have seen dogs save lives, but still stubbornly resist placing canine teams on their priority resource list. In my opinion, the dog resource should be used wisely and regularly. As with other SAR team components, dogs may be just the ticket or simply one of the valuable support systems that work so effectively toward a brilliant team effort.

Mission Base Logistics—Dan Burnett

Unfortunately, it is rare to the human soul to enjoy the satisfaction of feeling valued. This is true even among volunteers; or perhaps I should say, especially among volunteers. Often the most valuable person—the MVP—around mission base is the individual who can convince the new and inexperienced members that their seemingly insignificant contribution is what keeps the gears greased.

Media vehicle at staging area for Mayflower Gulch, by Dan Burnett

We have each been guilty of failing to see the big picture because of our limited focus and personal agenda. To be sure, it is vital to find that avalanche victim, especially as time wanes and darkness approaches. However, many other considerations affect the logistical mix and must not be ignored:

- Safety of searchers.
- Media control.
- Political aspects of interagency relations; i.e., Sheriff, Fire Department, Ambulance, Highway Patrol, Helicopter, Ski Areas, Ski Patrol, and other SAR teams.
- Weather and increasing risk.
- Reporting parties.
- Adrenaline pumped people, searchers and civilians alike.

Every additional person, including rescue dog teams, adds an increasing element of complication exponentially.

Missions typically run smoothest when those in authority have trained to the highest and most current level of Incident Command. Combine this consideration with selecting leaders who have the necessary experience and logistical skills required for avalanche SAR, and mission base can be a beautiful thing to behold.

More likely though, your first dozen experiences at mission base were downright confusing, and the irritability constituent tipped the scale. Try to keep in mind that, despite outward appearances, those "crazed" individuals with the radios attached to their ears all have the welfare of the victims as their foremost consideration. Hard to believe, isn't it? It is very likely that you, as avalanche dog handlers, have no clue how many different plates Command has to juggle at any given moment.

From a mission coordinator's point of view, dog handlers need to have tough skin if they are going to survive the mission base "adventure." Make a point of introducing yourself to whoever is the "boss," or a person who has been designated as the rescue dog liaison, and be ready for the minute when you will be deployed. Also, realize that you just may have to wait more than that minute. Because of safety or transportation deliberations, your wait may prove to be hours, rather than minutes. Come prepared for that eventuality.

Many good dog handlers have dropped out because they could not manage the stress that is inevitable in the multi-dimensional, ever-dynamic mission base.

Three attitudinal approaches, if adopted, will assure your success in dealing with the mission base "powers that be."

Attitude of Teachability	No one wants to be around a know-it-all. Determine that you can learn from the sheriff and firefighters; and consequently, they will figure out that you are an individual they can work with. This attitude helps alleviate the frustration that results from feeling that no one appreciates you for the "know-it-all" that you are.

Attitude of Service	You will be valued beyond imagination once you have proved that your goal is to serve the victim, the victim's friends and family, and the rescue community. Mission Base, even during major ICS operations, is not so bad if your approach is that you are there to serve others, rather than yourself.
Attitude of Incredible Good Fortune	The majority of people today live out their adventure fantasies by watching television and movies, playing video games, and reading books. You are incredibly blessed to have landed a leading role in a true-life mystery series. Mission Base affords you the opportunity to make a difference in the lives of other people in very significant ways.

It takes many years, with more than a few missions under your belt, before you have the opportunity to move up through the Command ranks. If you seriously choose to embrace your rescue dog responsibilities, in just a few years you will be provided front-line search action. Make the most of each opportunity and grow from your successes and your failures. If you prove to be a good resource to Mission Base, they will prove to be a good resource for you.

Who knows? You may even decide that in your next SAR career, you will want to be the one who wears the orange COMMAND vest and be the object of everyone else's frustration.

Proving the Worth of Avalanche Dogs

Expect to encounter agencies that do not acknowledge the value of SAR dogs. To some people, the use of rescue dogs for avalanche search is as absurd as divining rods or seers. Many SAR dog handlers expend an enormous amount of time and energy trying to make believers out of the skeptics.

Snow safety produced avalanche on Jacques Peak, Copper Mountain, By Dan Moroz

Some ski areas that have had avalanche accidents within their boundaries continue to deny a need for ski patrol dogs. When the demand arises, they prefer to call dogs from surrounding ski areas or search and rescue groups. Some ski area managers maintain understandable fear that perhaps a dog will run after a guest and either bite them or cause them to fall; but face it, some people just dislike or are afraid of dogs. I know of search and rescue groups that will spend days probing before they will call a local SAR group for dog assistance. By that time, the best one can hope for is a body recovery.

No amount of arguing or letter writing will influence these "Doubting Thomases." They must see an avalanche dog in action before they will be convinced. When the time comes to demonstrate how wonderful your dog is, you had better make darn sure that both you and your dog know your stuff—and know it well.

Aids in Better Utilization of Avalanche Dogs

Please realize that, other than rescue beacons, avalanche dogs are the buried victim's best hope for survival. Be aware of the various methods for deploying dog teams in your immediate area. Normally, the operational teams are easily accessed through the local county dispatcher or the ski patrol dispatchers. Many handlers carry pagers 24-7 through their SAR team or SAR dog team. Most of the ski area dogs remain at Patrol Headquarters during the day and are readily accessed via pre-determined landing zones on the top of the mountain.

Since time is the ultimate enemy to a person fighting for every breath of air, rapid transportation of rescue dog teams is essential. The use of helicopters, snow-cats, snowmobiles, and chairlifts are facilitated to get to the avalanche site. Dogs have very sensitive noses; that's why you called them in the first place. Help to protect those noses by having fuel operated vehicles and equipment positioned in an area well off the avalanche debris and downwind.

If there is a need to perform control work before searchers can enter the search area, dog teams should be on standby in the unlikely event that a snow safety worker is buried in a subsequent slide.

Avalanche dog teams expect to work alongside other searchers. While there is even the slightest hope of finding a live victim, leave every resource on the search area at the same time that the dogs are working. They train to work through distractions.

When a search goes into multiple days, allow the dogs to begin searching at first light, about 30 to 60 minutes before placing other resources on the slide area. This gives the dogs the added advantage of working a fresh area that has had all evening to decontaminate. The other benefit is that there is more scent diffusion first thing in the morning, when the air is colder.

Thoroughly instruct rescuers in SAR dog etiquette. They must never call to the dog while it is working, trying to get the dog to search a certain area or trying to play with it. The only person giving commands to the dog is the handler. Searchers should not contaminate the slide area by urinating, spitting, throwing trash, or leaving their own equipment in undesignated locations. Never, ever feed a rescue dog without express instructions from the handler.

If the dog team has not arrived with its own probe member, provide a person who can remain with the handler during the entire search period. The handler's primary objective is to read even the subtlest alerts that the dog provides. The assistant probes the alerts that the handler calls out and provides assistance with any other needs the team has. Keep in mind that a dog alert is always probed before it is shoveled. shoveling can waste valuable time, especially in the case of deep burials.

Critical Incident Stress Management

It is difficult to assess how each dog handler will respond to the stress of finding a person who has met an early death. We would like to think that we are all adults and can handle our emotions as well as the next SAR person, but critical incident stress (CIS) can take its toll if not handled correctly and promptly. A critical incident is any situation encountered by emergency responders that results in intense emotional repercussions. These feelings have the potential to incapacitate EMS workers to the point where they are no longer fit to perform their responsibilities.

Some of the normal reactions to CIS are fatigue, insomnia, hyperactivity, problem-solving difficulties, fear, guilt, depression, and anxiety.

Every SAR and ski patrol team should have at its disposal a Critical Incident Stress Management Team. Missions that have the potential to solicit CIS are deaths, mass casualties, and injury or death to a fellow EMS worker or a child. The team is comprised of a mental health clinician as well as one or two peers. In our case, the peers are either SAR or ski patrol members.

Good ways to cope with CIS are strenuous physical exercise, talking through your feelings with other rescue personnel, journaling, sufficient sleep, and good nutrition. This is one time when it is essential for you to be good to yourself.

> "The joys and heartaches are real, they are deep, and they are lasting. Sometimes the emotional aftermath of missions can destroy families and, perhaps unexpectedly, the lives of the searcher. Sometimes these emotions can be the thread that keeps them together, but they are never neutral and they rarely go away."
> —By Susan Bulanda, from *Ready to Serve; Ready to Save*. Page 9

Hasty and bronze statue of Hasty with sculptor, Brian Howard.

11 Public Relations & Avalanche Awareness

Expect High Visibility

An avalanche dog team needs to be constantly on its best behavior. SAR dogs bring more visibility and attention to you than you would like most of the time. People are watching to see how obedient your dog is, how your dog relates to other dogs and people, and whether your dog fools around or gets down to business on missions.

Lynne Engelbert working disaster dog, Lucy, at the World Trade Center terrorist attack, By Lynne Engelbert

Copper Mountain Ski Patrol avalanche dog teams, By Cullen Lyle

The media is constantly filming the dogs and attempting to interview their handlers, as was the case with the September 11 World Trade Center and Pentagon terrorist attacks. As I watched the disaster dog teams at work, I was proud of their stamina, dexterity, and perseverance. Ask yourself whether your actions will reflect positively or negatively on all SAR dogs in general.

Lectures

Do not miss the opportunities that your avalanche dog affords you to educate people about avalanche hazards and safety. Your dog is your key to an attentive audience especially with children. Over the years Hasty, Sandy, and I have spoken to Doctors, Nurses, Boy Scouts, Court Reporters, Ski Clubs, School Groups, Ski Patrols, and SAR Groups. I am constantly amazed at the numbers of people who are interested in learning more about our wonderful canine partners.

Ski Area PR

The ski areas have figured out that by allowing the press to film avalanche dog demonstrations, they get free advertising. Since most ski areas have at least one dog on duty every day, they do not need much advanced notice to pull off a great ski area public relations piece.

Fund Raising

Search and Rescue dogs are an expensive hobby, even for professional ski patrollers who usually still have to absorb all of the nutritional and medical expenses of their canine partners. I will not even try to estimate the cost to volunteers. The greatest investment is time away from work; then add to that food, travel, equipment, and veterinarian bills.

Sniagrab Poster, By Cindy Lee

People love to give to worthwhile causes and they love to give to animals. Find organizations that are willing to donate to your group when you give an avalanche dog presentation. With very little imagination, you should be able to come up with fund raising innovations.

> Garts Sports set up a snow cone booth at their annual Sniagrab (Bargains backward.) All of the proceeds went to the Copper Mountain Avalanche Dogs.

SAR Competitions

While SAR dog competition in Europe is a common occurrence, it has been a hot topic in the United States over the last few years. Recently I had to reflect on my motivation for participating in such an event. The promoters of "The Incredible Dog Challenge" approached me to help coordinate an avalanche dog competition in Breckenridge, Colorado. Initially, I questioned the merits of such an event. Concerned about my own human nature, I did not want to compete unless my incentive was to elevate avalanche dog awareness and not my particular dog.

Paul and Cathy Carson, the promoters, showed me footage of past events and the attitudes of the handlers and canines impressed me the most. Whether Agility, Sled, Diving, Frisbee, or Pole & Paw, the athletes, both winners and losers, were consumed with the joy of doing what they enjoyed most. There was camaraderie, exchange of training advice, and the thrill of better educating others via ESPN and national and local networks about the different canine events.

So, I agreed and we proceeded with the plans. Unlike Agility and Frisbee, with SAR competition, it was a challenge to try to even the playing fields. However, one detail emphasized throughout the event and TV production was that the competition was between the athletes—the dogs.

The competitors are all active members of a SAR or ski patrol organization and are fully operational/certified with their teams. At any given time one dog can have a bad day or receive a search area with more distractions, and consequently register a slower time. That dog is probably no less proficient than the dog that happened to win the particular event. Fortunately, our dogs do not have egos like ours; they are not glory seekers: "they just wanna have fun." They are out there doing what they love most, and that love and excitement is readily conveyed and contagious to the spectators and viewers. I love it when the public gets a better grasp of the incredible abilities of our canine partners. Face it; few people ever have the opportunity to watch a SAR dog operate.

I am not sure that we will ever completely see eye to eye about the legitimacy of these competitions, but think twice before criticizing a fellow dog handler. Perhaps we can politely agree to disagree. Otherwise, it will detract from our main goal, which is to work for the good of those we serve, those in serious need of our help. If you, as a SAR dog handler, ever have the opportunity to compete, try it. Maybe you will still feel the same way; but just maybe, your opinion will change.

12 Missions

Cottonwood Creek, Colorado—P. Burnett

Scenario: The weather in the Collegiate Range of the Colorado Rockies had been predominantly clear, cold, and windy. February 3 and 4 seemed like the perfect weekend to get out and enjoy the snowy backcountry.

Accident: Dan's wife watched as her husband used his snowmobile to highmark a steep slope near Lost Lake with his dog along for the ride. I am sure she must have stared in unbelief as a wall of snow suddenly enveloped him and the dog. She attempted to find Dan, who had no rescue beacon, and eventually had to go out for help.

Search: Rescuers from Chaffee County SAR responded with the only rescue dog available, a retired avalanche dog. When the fatigued searchers finally left the field after dark at 9:00 PM, they were still unsuccessful. At that point, they called for reinforcements.

Sunday morning at 8:30, a full-scale search operation was mounted, as 45 additional searchers and two rescue dogs proceeded up the appropriately named Avalanche trailhead to the site north of Lost Lake at an elevation of 11,000 feet.

Without much of a last seen point, we had very little in the way of alerts until about 2:30 PM. Tom and his avalanche dog, Donner, were working the toe of the slide when Donner began digging. To confirm his suspicions, his handler, TR, probed the area and got a strike. Dan was buried under five and a half feet of snow, in a face down position. His inverted machine was less than five feet away.

Slide Statistics: The avalanche had run between 1500 and 2000 feet vertically and was about a quarter of a mile wide. The deposition was 10 to 20 feet deep. *Note: for more detailed information regarding any of these slides, please access the Colorado Avalanche Information Center at http://geosurvey.state.co.us/avalanche or Westwide Avalanche Network at www.avalanche.org/.*

Lessons Learned:

- We theorized that the reason it took so long for the dogs to alert on the victim's body was the strong odor of gas fumes. The fuel had completely emptied out of the snowmobile and saturated the snow surrounding Dan's body. By mid-afternoon, the gases had dissipated enough to allow some scent from the body to reach the surface. We never did locate the buried dog. Train around snowmobiles so that your dog learns how to discriminate human scent from fumes.

- Snowmobilers must be equipped with rescue beacons, shovels, and a healthy understanding of avalanche safety.

- Each SAR group that is responsible for avalanche prone mountains should have at least one avalanche dog team readily available.

- Our experience is that many people who die in avalanches are in a prone, face down, position.

- Snowmobile victims are frequently found close to their machines.

This very same day a snowboarder died in an avalanche in the Steep Gullies, near Loveland Pass, Colorado.

Diamond Peak, Colorado—Jim Vail and P. Burnett

Note: Jim and Pepper, members of the Routt County SAR team and SARDOC, reside in Steamboat Springs, Colorado. Jim has ten years of experience in search and rescue dog handling. Pepper is a nine-year-old tenacious rescue dog, certified in wilderness airscent, water, and avalanche search—avalanche is her favorite. Jim especially enjoys mentoring young and developing SAR dog handlers and their puppies. He loves their focus and willingness to learn.

Scenario: The winter season commenced with very little snowfall, creating a significant depth hoar problem. Weather over the last 24 to 36 hours included cold temperatures, with wind chills of minus 40 to 50, and winds of 15 mph, with gusts upwards of 35 mph. Each day brought an increased avalanche hazard, as new snow accumulated in the starting zones, especially in the Diamond Peaks area. The Colorado Avalanche Information Center rated the hazard as moderate with pockets of high.

Accident: Cameron Pass, at times resembling a ski area, is very popular with backcountry enthusiasts, especially the local student populace. Twenty-one year old Daniel was studying wildlife biology at Colorado State University. While telemark skiing with some snowboarding friends on December 14, 1999, Daniel took an alternate route in order to skin up the south summit of Diamond Peak.

Search: At 1:30 p.m., when Daniel did not show up at the predetermined site, his friends began to worry. They soon discovered a fresh debris field close to where Daniel had been headed. In retrospect, one of the friends remembered that he had heard what he thought might have been the sound of an avalanche.

Daniel's friends began the rescue effort immediately, searching for him with every piece of equipment they had. Relentlessly, they probed and shoveled with their inadequate snowboards. After a few hours, they went out for help and were able to track down some United States Forest Service staff. Eight people performed a probe of the area, again with no results. The search was finally postponed for the evening due to decreasing visibility, below zero wind chill temperatures, and increasing wind loading.

The second day dawned cold and cloudy on Cameron Pass, and a lazy old bull moose watched as 20 searchers and five avalanche dog teams from Routt, Larimer, Vail, and Summit Counties were briefed near the Diamond Peak trailhead. Jim was excited because it was his first opportunity to field with Pepper, his Border Collie/Australian Cattle Dog mix, who had been avalanche certified for two years. While skinning in to the area, the snowpack collapsed on a number of occasions.

The Diamond Peak Nordic Patrol was responsible for determining the stability of the area. It was their weighty judgment whether rescuers could enter the field. My navigator, Tim, a ski patroller and dog handler, was able to assist them in the snowpack evaluation. While making the assessment, the hasty search team also performed a beacon search.

Tim discovered a distinct skinning up track, possibly made by Daniel. The track entered the debris three-fourths of the way up the slide path. While all the searchers waited, Tim and Sarah, from Diamond Peak Ski Patrol, performed hasty pits and ski cutting to mitigate any remaining hang-fire. They decided that if rescuers remained on the deposition and slide path, the risk would be minimal.

Once the hasty team completed their assignments, the dog teams started simultaneously near the toe of the deposition. There were a number of areas where dogs showed interest; these may have been places were skis and poles were buried. They also showed curiosity in holes that searchers had dug out the previous evening.

SARDOC dog, pepper, working an avalanche, By Jim Vail

Since most of the dogs were on the deepest part of the debris, Jim decided to direct Pepper lower, near the edge of the toe. At 10:35 a.m., about ten yards from the toe and just ten minutes after starting, Pepper aggressively dug down to a glove. Jim at first thought that his dog had discovered another clue. As he bent down to look at the glove, Pepper began digging in another area about three feet away—she had uncovered a telemark boot. Jim yelled, "We have a find." This was the first time Pepper had alerted so enthusiastically on a deceased victim. "Good girl." Sandy then pulled at the glove, which exposed Daniel's hand.

The young man was lying on his back, across the hill with his head slightly lower than his feet. He did not have any of his skis or poles, but his backpack was still in place. Obvious signs of trauma included a 2" long scalp laceration over his left eye and some lower leg deformity. There was barely any snow in his mouth, nose, or ears and a half-inch thick ice lens surrounded Daniel's face. One of his hands and one of his boots were close to the surface. The coroner's office listed a severed spinal cord as the cause of death; Daniel had sustained a broken neck. This young man was the first avalanche fatality of the season.

Slide Statistics: The elevation of the avalanche was approximately 11,400' with an east, northeast aspect. The fracture line was 18 to 24" deep and 75 yards wide. The slide traveled about 200 yards long on a weak layer that was 14" above the ground. There were five to six distinct layers in the snowpack. The debris was 150 by 200 yards, with a depth of two to five feet. The avalanche was soft slab and Daniel, most likely, triggered it himself. I remember remarking how easy it was to dig through the debris.

Lessons Learned:
- These young men were not prepared. It is difficult enough trying to probe and dig with equipment specially designed for that purpose. Skis, conventional ski poles, and snowboards are even more ineffective and cumbersome.

- I was glad that we had trained with gloves as a reward. Sandy was given the most positive of rewards in this mission.

- Daniel's friends were prudent in looking for him before going out for help. When avalanche victims are located alive, it is usually because their friends begin searching immediately.

- Daniel was smart to have detached his ski poles straps from around his wrists. When caught in a slide, it is important to get rid of any equipment (backpacks, skis, and poles) that can drag a person deeper into the deposition. One of the disadvantages of telemark and snowboard equipment is that most people do not use releasable bindings.

- It appeared that Daniel was trying to reach his hand toward the surface, a wise move had he been skiing with companions…and had he not suffered a broken neck.

- Never, ever ski in the backcountry alone. Ski parties should remain together. Two heads are better than one, and two rescue beacons are better than one. One transmitting beacon alone is usually only good enough for a body recovery.

- We were careful to make sure that all of the dogs had an opportunity to dig down to Daniel—an invaluable tool in their training for future avalanche searches.

- Whenever possible, respond with your own navigator/prober/snow safety technician. Another mind and set of eyes is beneficial when determining the efficacy of entering the field.

As Jim put it so well, "We continue to practice, hoping that we never have to find another dead person, but being prepared just in case."

Factory Hill, Yellowstone National Park— B. Gafney

Note: Bonnie Gafney, employed with the National Park Service since 1979, has worked SAR dogs since 1989, the last eight years with the Western Montana Search Dogs Team. Bonnie and her dogs train in avalanche, wilderness, and cadaver search, and her dogs have been credited with many finds throughout Montana, Wyoming, Idaho, and some of the other National Parks. Bonnie's dog, Sarena, had a ten-year career in SAR, and after retirement, turned her harness over to Smokey.

Scenario: Here are the facts about the avalanche in Yellowstone National Park (YNP) that took the lives of two people on March 3, 1997. The victims of this fatal incident were Rick Hutchinson, YNP Geologist, and Diane Dustman, VIP.

Accident: The avalanche probably took place mid-morning Monday, March 3. Rick radioed in at 8:00 a.m., indicating his intent to leave some seismic equipment on the top of Paycheck Pass to lighten his load for the ski out the next day. He cautioned us about avalanche concerns on Factory Hill, which had sustained a large slide in early December. Weekend storms brought 20" of snow with strong, gusting winds.

Search: Uncharacteristically, Rick did not check in that evening. The next day, Tuesday, Rick and Diane did not show up along the trail, where they had planned to meet another ski group. This group noticed two recent avalanches on Factory Hill. They hurried to the cabin where they found all of Rick and Diane's gear, including the radio. Both sets of skis were gone, including Rick's frame pack. Radioing in, they returned to the slide area in the dark but safety concerns prevented any more than a hasty search. Ski tracks were located leading in and out of one slide, but only leading into the second and larger slide. An organized search and rescue effort was initiated.

On Wednesday, three dog teams flew in from Jackson, WY. Snowmobile experts from West Yellowstone SAR broke trail into Paycheck Pass, also shuttling in a fourth dog team from YNP. During this time, a number of backcountry experts from Teton National Park and the Jackson Ski Area did a fly-over to assess the situation. They concluded that a high avalanche risk remained from the hang-fire above the accident site. Searchers were restricted from the area until they deployed 175 pounds of explosives to strategic places. No new avalanches occurred, and the area was deemed safe for the three dog teams that were waiting. The fourth team and 12 probers continuing in, taking Rick's routine route to Heart Lake, through a thermal area that stretched along Witch Creek.

Once on the scene, a probe line was organized while the four dog teams worked the debris randomly. The ski tracks leading into the larger slide were extrapolated out, and primary search efforts were focused from there to the toe of the slide. Dog teams had subtle alerts, which were followed up with frequent probing, verification by other dog teams, and shoveling. There were no conclusive dog alerts at this time. Weather included strong gusty winds, with variable clouds and snow squalls. At dusk, efforts were postponed and all of the teams left the field.

On Thursday morning two fresh dog teams were flown in from Jackson Hole and the YNP dog team was flown in from the staging area. Weather was partly cloudy to clear, with minimal winds and temperatures in the teens. These teams began a corridor search of the debris, switching positions periodically to check each other's work. Two teams located animal remains about two and a half feet deep near the toe of the small slide. Comprehensive probing was performed for even the subtlest alerts. There were no strong indications, other than the animal locations, which the dogs left easily.

A second YNP dog team responded to Paycheck Pass, from where they walked down to search the thermal area. They located older ski and foot tracks, believed to be Rick and Diane's, with no indication of any recent activity. Temperatures approached 30 degrees, with small snow squalls and gusting winds.

At 4:30 p.m. Thursday, the probe line located Rick's body under four feet of dense snow, approximately 30 feet above the proposed ski route. He was encrusted by an ice lens, and facing uphill. One ski and both ski poles were missing. By all outward appearances, trauma was not a factor in the cause of death. Eventually, probers also located one ski pole about 20 feet below Rick's body. Dogs and probers made an intense effort to locate Diane's body in the same area. However, at 5:30 p.m., search operations were suspended for the day due to imminent darkness and continued blowing snow. All teams left the scene via helicopter, snowmobiles, and snowshoes.

The search resumed Friday, with one YNP dog team and a new patrol team from Bozeman, Montana. At 12:30 p.m., a probe line located Diane's body under about seven and a half feet of snow, approximately 50 feet above where Rick's body had been found. Her legs had penetrated the dense deadfall from December's avalanche debris.

Not one of the eight certified dog teams alerted in the areas where the bodies were discovered. Only two dogs even showed interest after they were unburied. One of those dogs knew Rick well, and once she nudged him, she realized who he was. As can be expected, the involved dog handlers were concerned and frustrated. Throughout the search, we had strategized frequently, puzzled by the absence of significant alerts. All of the teams were experienced, some having had other avalanche finds. All of the teams worked with obvious purpose and intent.

Lessons Learned:

- The winter of 1996-97 was a record snow year, with 96" on the ground stake at Grant Village. Unusual snowfall accumulations bring unusual avalanche cycles.

- Forest fires in 1998 left Factory Hill covered with burned timber. The December 1996 slide was possibly the first avalanche to occur in the area. The avalanche wiped the hillside clean, many of the trees swept, matchstick style, into Witch Creek. Snow anchors were rare.

- Factory Hill derives its name from the constant splashing, roaring, and steaming that resembles an old steam works. Geyser activity is most intense near the upper end of the Fissure Group. Witch Creek flows through the center of that group, and consists of thermal runoff with temperatures of 85 degrees F. The base of Factory Hill is usually devoid of snow, yet was covered with avalanche debris during this particular winter.

- Some of the thermal features were covered with debris, mostly from the December slide, establishing snow bridges over the logs and creating gas pockets and tunnels beneath the snow, at places two feet deep. Over the tunnels, a layer of firm, icy snow indicated that the snow was melting from the bottom up. This phenomenon was most apparent below the toe of the avalanche. Searchers even broke through, landing on logs, four and five deep that were lying on mushy, smelly earth.

- When the dogs failed to locate the bodies, we expanded the search area, thinking that they may have been pushed into a sinkhole below the toe. Later, searchers discovered a strong smell of sulfur in the hole where Diane was found. She may have fallen through one of the soft "sinkholes," possibly causing the avalanche that took their lives.

- The snow and ground temperatures at the site were significantly warmer than normal, a further indication of strong thermal influence. The affected area contained the highest concentration of TG snow found anywhere in the area.

- Several SAR personnel on the scene experienced sore and raspy throats with nasal congestion during and after the incident. Sulfur and hydrogen dioxide gases are associated with thermal activity. The smell of sulfur is extremely unpleasant, but hydrogen dioxide is odorless and far more toxic; it can anesthetize the nasal tissues in humans. Rick, one of our victims, no longer had a "sense of smell" after all his years in the geyser basins. Certainly, this would have been a factor in the dogs' olfactory abilities.

- The dog handlers from the Yellowstone National Park search wondered what they might have done to their dogs by asking them to participate in this mission.

Fourth Steep Gully, Colorado—P. Burnett

> "Despite warnings of extreme avalanche danger, a skier and snowboarder were killed in separate backcountry snow slides Tuesday, pushing the state closer to dubious record."
> —*Denver Post*, January 26, 2000

Scenario: Following an already moist weather cycle, 40 more inches of snow fell on the Colorado Rockies, and an avalanche warning was issued. Meanwhile, a snowshoer from Denver was buried in the Jones Pass area near Berthoud Pass on Sunday. While her friends were able to dig themselves out, they had no equipment for her extrication.

Just three days later, a Snowmass skier was killed in the Little Annie Basin, on the backside of Aspen Mountain, bringing the season's avalanche death toll to five. Unfortunately, white death had not finished reaping its harvest that day.

> "To be honest, I can't think of a worse place that anyone could have been today, and there were a lot of bad places."
> —Scott Toepfer, Colorado Avalanche Information Center

Accident: The skiing conditions in-bounds were the best they had been all winter. Unfortunately, there are those outdoor enthusiasts who are always pursuing a greater challenge. Five Summit County snowboarders, in their early 20's, were having a great time flirting with chance on Tuesday, January 25. They had already triggered one slide in the steep gullies, also known locally as "The Beavers," outside of Arapaho Basin Ski Area's boundary.

Search: Around noon, they again decided to push their luck. This time they were not so fortunate. One of them was buried, but, without the benefit of beacons or shovels, his friends were unable to find him. Finally, one of the friends made his way out to the road and flagged down a commercial truck driver, who reported the avalanche to the Arapaho Basin Ski Patrol.

The initial response included an Arapaho Basin Ski Patrol Snow Safety Team, assigned to reduce further avalanche danger to the rescuers. The snowpack was so tender that as they traversed in to the area, without throwing any explosives, they triggered an additional slide. Once they eliminated the hangfire, the patrollers began their hasty search. They noticed a curious trail of blood and assumed that the victim's body was probably lower in the deposition than the blood. Another assumption was that one of the friends injured himself during the initial search efforts. Their probing resulted in no strikes.

Thirty minutes later, rescuers from the Summit County Rescue Group and other patrollers from Arapaho Basin, Keystone, Breckenridge, and Copper Mountain trudged into the area with four avalanche dogs. Searchers concentrated their efforts primarily in an area below the trail of blood.

John Reller was on scene with his two Golden Retrievers, Skadee and Pager. John started both dogs working in the most likely area. He observed as his younger dog, Pager, on her own initiative, worked up the slide path until she began digging around a tree. She found the buried man close to the surface, perhaps only six to twelve inches deep. Wrapped backwards, around a tree, he had

Summit county rescue group handler and Copper Mountain ski patroller, John Reller, By Dan Burnett

sustained serious head, back, and hip trauma. The violence inflicted upon this young man's body was incomprehensible.

> In studying the history of avalanches in this particular area of Summit County, I remembered that a very similar accident occurred on March 13, 1982. A 30-year-old Breckenridge man was buried under three feet of snow. The mission report indicated that he was bent backwards around the tree, with his feet only inches from his head. Over the years, the backcountry community has memorialized this man for his life's motto: "SKI TO DIE!"

Lessons Learned:

- Never presume that rescue beacons and shovels are optional equipment. Never leave home without them.

- Most avalanches occur during and following storm cycles. This is the best time to frequent the ski areas.

- Give the backcountry snowpack an opportunity to stabilize.

- Heed the warnings of the avalanche information centers. They are an invaluable resource.

- Twenty-something men should read the statistics. It is not in their favor to wink at the numbers. Never approach backcountry skiing as a game of chance.

- It is vital that ski patrols and search and rescue groups train and preplan together closely. The resources these agencies afford each other are indispensable.

- Safety is a major consideration in operating a search. Control any remaining hazard before allowing rescuers onto the slide path.

- Blood is an unusual phenomenon in avalanche deposition, unless one of the rescue dogs has cut a pad. Our experience in this particular search was that the victim's body was found above the blood. The snow, as it traveled past his suspended body, collected blood and carried it down lower.

"People are taking ridiculous risks. Their friends and families are going to suffer forever for the thrill they are chasing after today."
—Dan Burnett, Summit County Rescue Group

Francie's Cabin, Colorado—P. Burnett

Scenario: On Saturday, January 15, 1995, Dr. Ken was skiing in the backcountry near Breckenridge, Colorado. The 33-year-old physician at the Children's Hospital Emergency Department was in excellent health and an experienced backcountry skier. He had decided to check out Francie's Cabin, since he and his friends had booked the hut for a later date. He stopped by the cabin for lunch, leaving at 1:30 p.m. The people, who spoke with Dr. Ken as he left the hut, thought he was heading back down the trail to return home. Instead, he must have decided to get a few more turns in before hitting the road.

That evening at approximately 10 p.m., his new wife of six months became concerned and dialed 911 to report Ken's failure to return home. Unfortunately, she did not have any information as to his whereabouts, only that he was cross-country skiing somewhere up in the county. The Summit County Sheriff's Department began a search for the missing man's car. Given the myriad of trailheads in the area, they were unable to locate his vehicle that night.

> "About 50 times a year, people will call and say a friend is lost in Summit County. Our volunteers can't go until they get more precise information about where to begin searching."
> —From Dan Burnett, SCRG Mission Coordinator

Sunday morning authorities learned that Dr. Ken might have been skiing in an area approximately two and a half miles south of Breckenridge near Francie's Cabin, a cabin in the Summit Huts and Trails system. His car was discovered in the Watson lot, not the customary parking place for Francie's

Accident: At about 11:30 a.m., Dispatch received a cell phone call from a guest at Francie's Cabin describing a slide they could see a third of a mile southwest of the hut above Crystal Creek. There appeared to be tracks going into the avalanche, with none coming out. At about 11 a.m., other guests from the cabin had skied up to the slide to probe it with their ski poles and skis.

Search: The Avalanche Deployment Program mobilized immediately. Our family had just returned from church, and Hasty and I responded the short distance to the Medical Center's LZ, where the Flight for Life helicopter was standing by. We flew over the deposition and saw that people were still probing the area. There was no significant avalanche danger, and we felt comfortable about beginning a search.

Hasty and I were dropped off about 300 yards from the slide. Since the snow was uncompacted, the ship hovered as Hasty and I jumped out, immediately sinking up to our hips, my hips—his neck, in fresh snow. Meanwhile, other SCRG members responded via personal vehicles, SAR trucks, and snowmobiles. Skadee, another avalanche dog, responded from Copper Mountain where she was on duty. All told, nearly 30 individuals assisted in the rescue efforts.

Once I got my telemark skis on, we traversed the short distance to the deposition. I started Hasty working and he began digging within seconds. I asked the probers to check that area while I continued working my dog into the wind. A few minutes later, he gave me a stronger alert and this time dug

Patti helping Hasty dig down to the subject, By Dan Burnett

frantically. At 1 p.m., we achieved a strike and dug down to the young doctor's lifeless body.

According to his tracks, Dr. Ken carefully picked his way through the trees, avoiding the steeper, starting zone. He may have assumed that since the higher area did not slide, the lower portion of the path was safe. It appeared from the tracks into the slide, that the slope broke loose about 100' above him, carrying him 50-75'. It is postulated that Dr. Ken was killed instantly. His body came to rest near the slide's toe next to a stand of trees, a likely burial site. He was lying on his stomach under four feet of snow with his head facing downhill. Dr. Ken's skis were still attached and his poles were nearby. There was not an ice mask to indicate that he had died of suffocation necessarily. However, there was a pocket around his entire body, formed as his warm body melted the surrounding snow.

Thirty different rescuers from SCRG and the Summit County Sheriff's Office helped on this mission.

Slide Statistics:

The weather conditions before this accident were blowing and snowing. The terrain around Francie's Cabin was often "ripe for avalanches because of the strong winds," according to Knox Williams.

We had all experienced snowpack settlement while skiing to the avalanche, with no cracking or movement. Jim Repsher, from the Copper Mountain Ski Patrol, performed a fracture profile. He noticed two other slab avalanches on the same ridge that may have happened at the same time.

The slide had a 32-degree slope angle, with an east-northeast aspect, at an elevation of approximately 11,700'. The avalanche slid near the ground, on an old layer of snow. The slide was 300' (length) by 200' (vertical), hard slab to soft slab, with a depth of four to ten feet. Most of the debris chunks were about the size of grapefruits and easy to dig through, even after 18 hours. Dr. Ken was the third victim of avalanches that season. The other two died while hiking Belford in the Sawatch Range the previous October.

Lessons Learned:

- Never assume that just because the normal loading zone does not slide, the compression zone is safe. Strong winds can load snow lower on an avalanche slope, causing instability in the compression zone.

- This slide was not a huge one. People mistakenly think that they will be able to out-ski or out-ride a smaller slide. Perhaps we all watch too many extreme skiing movies. It is often the smaller, apparently benign, pockets that entrap the unsuspecting.

- To venture into avalanche terrain alone is risky business. Of the people who actually survive avalanche burials, they live because the members of their own party locate and unbury them.

- Carry an avalanche shovel and beacon and know how to use them.

- Rescue dog handlers should never put all your eggs into one basket, figuring that the avalanche dogs' first alert is the most accurate one they will get. Continue working the dog until it gives you the best indication. Do not waste precious time digging in places where a dog has only alerted faintly.

- Terrain selection is an important and indispensable skill when backcountry skiing. This proficiency comes from accompanying others who are experienced decision-makers about which slopes are safe and which are not. There is also no substitute for attending avalanche courses.

Marvin Gardens, Colorado—P. Burnett

Scenario: For a week, it had snowed nonstop, depositing more than two feet of snow in the Colorado Rockies. An avalanche fatality had occurred at Cameron Pass on Sunday. On Tuesday, January 13, 1993, after a night of hard blowing snow, the entire backcountry posed a huge threat. Little was needed to trigger new slides.

That same day, three Vail Ski Instructors left the ski area, passing warning signs, in their quest to ski the popular Marvin Gardens area. For the past six years, the friends regularly tested their backcountry skills, and one of them had even suffered an injured spleen the previous winter while taking an avalanche ride.

Accident: Before heading out of bounds, the trio stopped in at Vail's Patrol Headquarters to warm up. Patrollers warned the three of the dangers out in the East Vail Chutes. The group skied across numerous pockets of instability. Judging from the entry tracks, 32-year-old Howard must have jumped into the chute and triggered a small slide. All three of them were involved, but only Howard was completely buried.

Search: The buried man's friends searched for him for an hour or two, using ordinary ski poles and shovels, before skiing out to I-70 to solicit help at around 5:00 p.m. Subsequently, we were summoned to respond to the slide. About five Copper Mountain patrollers drove over to Vail to see if anything could be done that night. Since we could not get into the field before dark, we were asked to return the following morning at 8:30 a.m. for a National Guard helicopter ride.

Marvin Gardens is a huge bowl, filled with many different slide paths, that all dump down into a narrow chute. The Vail Ski Patrol was tasked with reducing any remaining hazards, which they promptly dispatched with 16 two and three pound charges via one of the helicopters.

Once the control work was completed, the other ship deposited us slightly above the avalanche that buried Howard. Within 10 or 15 minutes, Cache alerted 30 feet below the last seen point. Being Cache's first experience with a dead body, he urinated at that point and then promptly started digging. His handler, Todd, probed and got a strike.

Copper Mountain ski patroller, Todd Goertzen, Cache, Patti, and Hasty leaving Air National Guard helicopter, By Bill Mcdonald

By 11:40 a.m., we were able to dig the body out from under five feet of snow. There was an ice mask about ¾" thick around the victim's face.

The day after the Marvin Gardens accident, a 23-year-old snowboarder was killed while riding an out-of-bounds area at Ski Sunlight. In this case, the reporting party would not indicate exactly where the avalanche occurred because he did not want to get in trouble for cutting the ski area boundary. Ironically, his friend died with a hand sticking out of the snow. Think people!

"Their deaths, ironically, occurred during Colorado's annual Avalanche Awareness Week."
—Written by Kevin McCullen, *Rocky Mountain News*

Slide Statistics: The slide was about 300 yards across and had been partially covered by the avalanches produced by the control work. The bowl included 20 separate soft slab slides with fractures of 8 to 20 feet wide and three to four feet deep. Each of them ran about 150 to 250 feet in length. It was estimated that all of the slides combined measured about 1,000 feet across. The slide that killed Howard began on a 35 to 40 degree slope.

Lessons Learned:
- Avalanche transmitters and shovels are more than a good idea. They can save your life. As a human-interest point, all three men had purchased beacons and shovels for each other for Christmas. Unfortunately, the beacons were on back-order and arrived in the mail the day after the accident.

- For the right missions, helicopters are a great resource. This was that type of mission. Trying to get searchers in to the field any other way would have been lengthy and dangerous. This entire mission took a mere hour from start to finish because of the Air National Guard.

Montezuma, Colorado—P. Burnett

Scenario: The weekend was a particularly dangerous one for those who ventured into the backcountry. 26 inches of heavy, wet snow fell in 24 hours on top of older snow layers that did not have the strength to support the load. A hundred and one avalanches were reported between three p.m. Friday and three p.m. Sunday. The previous Thursday, two mountain bikers were caught in an avalanche near Keystone. The Colorado Avalanche Information Center posted a high hazard rating for the Montezuma area.

> "Mid-layers in the snowpack are still weak, especially on northern facing slopes. This will continue to be dangerous to backcountry travelers for the rest of the winter."
> —By a Forecaster with the CAIC

Accident: 28-year-old Takashi, a Japanese high school gymnastics and ski coach, was backcountry skiing with Montezuma Snowcat Tours on March 29, 1992. For six hours, the group received snowcat rides up the road, skiing the extreme terrain without incident. The guide carefully advised the nine clients which route to ski in the Equity Chute, but Takashi deviated slightly from the instructions. There was some question as to whether he fully understood the English language and the corresponding directions. At 3:30 p.m., the other clients watched as an avalanche carried the young man through the snow.

Search: They desperately tried to ascertain the place where they had seen him last. Realizing that most avalanche victims found alive are found by their own skiing party, the group sent one person out for help and used the remainder of the skiers to search for Takashi. The beacon search did not pick up any signals.

As with most confirmed burials, every available resource responded that Sunday afternoon. Four dog teams arrived from Arapahoe Basin, Keystone, and Copper Mountain. Unfortunately, they could not begin working until 7:00 p.m., for fear of more slides emptying further snow into our designated search area. Because of the encroaching darkness, there was no way to handle the remaining avalanche hazard adequately. Command decided that only a skeletal crew would venture out onto the debris; the group consisted of all the dogs, four handlers, and four probers.

Most of the snow in the avalanche was well consolidated, making travel easy. However, the preceding day's warm temperatures made the edges of the slide path difficult to navigate because of post-holing. The winds were primarily down-slope.

Hasty got an alert close to where we entered the deposition. Probers checked it but did not get a strike. An hour later, Skadee also indicated on the same position but more vigorously; again, no strike. After just an hour and a half, we were required to leave the deposition because of the diminishing light and exponentially increasing risk.

Rescuers digging down to a "Strike" in the equity chutes, By Dan Burnett

Monday morning we arrived at 7:00 a.m. to continue searching. The mutual agency response was overwhelming with SAR personnel arriving from Summit, Grand, and Alpine teams. Well over 40 searchers and three dog teams waited anxiously while a helicopter-guide company deployed explosives to stabilize the remaining snow in the avalanche chutes above the initial slide path. Fresh avalanches slid onto the area we had been searching the previous afternoon and early evening. It was sobering to imagine what could have happened if that slide had occurred at the same time that eight people and four dogs were searching.

Once we received the okay to resume our search, we sent the dogs onto the debris one at a time for 15 minutes each. Given the small dimensions of the slide, we agreed that this would be a good strategy. Hasty alerted about 40 feet above the alerts from the previous evening. He also gave his article indication on one of Takashi's buried ski poles.

A probe line ran directly between the strongest alerts and at 10:30 a.m. there was a strike. We surmised that the reason for the distance between the two alerts was the down-slope winds Sunday night and the up-slope winds Monday morning.

It wasn't until 11:30 a.m. that the young man's body was dug out from under ten and a half feet of snow. The violent ride ripped the beacon off his body and completely disabled it. Takashi was the fourth person to die in Colorado avalanches since February 25.

Slide Statistics: The avalanche occurred on a north-facing slope in Montezuma. Our search area was about 40 yards wide and 400 yards high, with debris as deep as 20 feet in places.

Lessons Learned:

- For those who have only skied within the ski area boundaries, the backcountry is a different animal. It can be thrilling and it can be dangerous. Guides' instructions must be followed explicitly as they have the skill and experience required for making the tough decisions.

- The eight snowcat guests were doing the right thing skiing one at a time, as directed by their guide.

- The victim's beacon was rendered inoperable. He may have been wearing it on the outside of his jacket—not a good idea. Make it a habit to carry your beacon in the inside pocket of your coat.

- Weigh the risk carefully and boldly declare any concerns you may have about entering unstable terrain.

- Teach your dog to alert on articles as well as live human scent. Every clue is important in search work. Of course, the most important "clue" is the victim.

- Always be aware of wind direction and speed. It directly affects the transport of scent within the snowpack, as well as in the air above the snowpack. As the wind increases in strength, the dog's alert is farther from the victim. This is also the case with burial depth. The deeper the burial, the farther the dog's alert will be from the victim.

- Avalanche deaths usually occur in cycles. While the temptation to explore the fresh powder is overwhelming, going into the backcountry is not a good idea when the media is reporting recent avalanche activity and accidents. Make it your business to check your local avalanche information center updates regularly.

Mt. Kelso, Colorado—P. Burnett

Scenario: On October 17, 1984, two Summit County men decided that, with the unseasonable October storm, they would try their backcountry skills on Mt. Kelso, a ridge north of Grays and Torreys Peak, accessible from Loveland Pass. It was unusual to find enough snow to ski extreme terrain this early in the season.

Accident: At around 1:00 p.m. Turbo triggered an avalanche that buried him. His friend, Dan, searched for a few hours before leaving the area to get help.

Search: Searchers from Alpine Rescue Team, Summit County Rescue Group, Loveland Ski Patrol, Flight for Life, and Clear Creek Sheriff's Department responded to the Bakersville command post.

After probing the deep debris for hours, at approximately 6:00 p.m., we discovered the young man's body beneath ten feet of snow. This was my first experience finding someone who had been killed in an avalanche. Although Turbo had been buried for at least five hours, our flight nurse ordered the initiation of CPR. Of the 20 rescuers present, I was the only one who volunteered to perform rescue breathing. My husband, Dan, said that everyone else took a step backwards. I had not noticed.

Those were the early days of CPR and today's universal precautions of facemasks and gloves were a protocol of the future. With each breath, I heard a gurgling noise and wondering what physiological phenomenon caused that sound. My SAR and medical experience were fast-forwarded that evening. After 20 minutes, we were directed to stop CPR.

I will never forget Turbo's girlfriends distraught face when she received the news. There was no consoling her. It all seemed such an utter waste. I wish that others who place their friends and family under similar anguish could have been there to witness the suffering that this avalanche death caused that October day.

Slide Statistics: The avalanche occurred in the primary path on the eastern aspect of Mount Kelso. The fracture line was two feet deep and the slide path was 1,000 feet long, traveling down a narrow gully. The deposition was 500 feet, top to bottom, and 20 to 30 feet wide.

Lessons Learned:
- Turbo's friend did the right thing in searching for him before skiing out for help.
- Always carry your own facemask should you have to perform CPR. Do not expect someone else to have the medical equipment you may need.
- With the assistance of an avalanche dog, we may have been able to find Turbo a lot faster. This was one incident in a chain of events that helped in my decision to begin a rescue dog program in Summit County.
- Avalanches can occur during any time of the year, especially in the high country. The earliest avalanche response we had done in the previous

seven years had been Thanksgiving. Early season snowfall may look attractive, but what you do not see can hurt you. Shallow, fall to mid-winter snow-packs have negligible stability and should be avoided unless a person is sure about their strength and cohesiveness.

Peak 7, Colorado—P. Burnett

Scenario: On Wednesday, February 18, 1987, the largest, most lethal avalanche accident occurred in the history of the Summit County Rescue Group. The place was the Peak 7 Bowl, just out of bounds from the Breckenridge Ski Area. To access this terrain, people skied past three warning signs advising of uncontrolled avalanche slopes. The Breckenridge Ski Area had just revised the wording of the signs, further warning of the inevitable avalanche risk. That day, the Colorado Avalanche Information Center had rated the danger as moderate, with pockets of instability warranting caution. Since December, there had been no major snowfall; then it finally started to snow.

Many people had been yo-yo skiing that winter day, riding the Breckenridge lifts, leaving the resort through the boundary ropes, skiing Peak 7, reentering the ski area, and riding the lifts again repeatedly.

Accident: Two skiers decided that they would hike to the top of the peak in order to gain elevation and a few extra turns, since everyone else had been taking a lower traverse into the bowl. At 2:04 p.m., ski patrollers and guests riding the Peak 8 T-Bar, witnessed two large avalanches that ran almost concurrently on the northern side of Peak 7. Nine skiers were involved in the accident, with four completely buried, two partially buried, and three just caught, but not buried.

Search: Considering the magnitude of this search operation, logistics and organization went very well. Breckenridge patrollers started a beacon search within 18 minutes of the time of the accident. According to Mary Logan, with the Breckenridge Ski Patrol, there were 83 volunteers within the first hour of the event. Rescuers were screened, and logged in and out as they entered and exited the field, respectively. People did not have long to wait for their assignments. Command immediately briefed them and designated them to teams.

Interagency cooperation was impressive. The Sheriff coordinated security and the media. Breckenridge Ski Patrol's management of the rescue effort was nothing less than outstanding. From the orange colored vests worn by the various officers, to the execution of normal rescue protocol, there was very little lacking. They had large maps posted on boards near the bottom of the deposition indicating clues, probed areas, location of found victims, dog alerts, places last seen, etc.

Command included the Summit County Sheriff's Office, Breckenridge Ski Patrol, and the Summit County Rescue Group. These were the days before the Incident Command System—at least as far as Summit County was concerned. Once unified command was in place, Dale Atkins became the Site Commander and Hunter Holloway, with the Colorado Search and Rescue Board, was the State Mission Coordinator. Other agencies that responded were Vail Mountain Rescue, Alpine Rescue Team, Grand County SAR, and all the local ski patrols.

Some of the equipment used for this mission included a helicopter, 4 snow-cats, 16 snowmobiles, 2 metal detectors, a ground radar unit, a command trailer, 2 ambulances, 130 probe poles, 2 tents, 2 generators, and 60 radios.

Three dog teams responded to the mission the first day. For Hasty and I, this was our first experience on a real mission; and to this day, Peak 7 is the largest avalanche I have ever searched. I was able to work Hasty for about three hours on Wednesday; and during that time, we had some false alerts. By 5:00 p.m., there were 200 rescuers on the deposition. At 5:15 p.m., a probe line located one of the victims beneath four feet of snow. At 6:00 p.m., darkness forced the suspension of operations.

On day two, 4 rescue dog teams and 300 probers waited as Colorado Heli-Ski assisted with avalanche control measures. Since by this time we were most likely dealing with body recoveries, command allowed the dogs to work the deposition for the first 30 minutes by themselves, free of distractions. Despite Hasty's youth and inexperience, he showed high motivation and energy during our ten and one half-hour workday. With so many volunteer members of the public on scene, I had to ask the site commander to prohibit people from urinating, spitting tobacco, and tossing food and wrappers onto the deposition. Close to noon, probers and metal detectors found the second and third victims buried four and seven feet deep.

By the third day, Hasty and three dogs from Rocky Mountain Rescue Dogs (RMRD) in Utah responded. At this late stage in the search, we realized that two generator-warmed tents were directly upwind of the deposition area. These tents were being used to warm cold rescuers as well as for the coroner's duties. The generator fumes saturated the deposition, making it nearly impossible for the dogs to find scent. We had the tents relocated on the last day, and were able to get a positive alert on the remaining body.

Hasty alerted at a position high on the deposition. Initially, the coarse probe was unsuccessful. However, Hasty and another dog from RMRD refused to leave the area when we attempted to redirect them. The second probe of the area resulted in a strike. After six hours, we located the final victim under three feet of snow. He was only 30 feet from the top of the deposition. All of the victims had died of traumatic asphyxiation.

> "Fifty emergency agencies from across the State expended a total of 344 man-days or 6169 man-hours on this mission."
> —By Tom Randolph, taken from Summit County Rescue Group, 25 Years, page 4-77

Immediately following the mission, the Sheriffs Office, the US Forest Service, and the County Offices met to discuss ski area boundary management concerns.

Slide Statistics: One or two skiers triggered the initial combination hard slab, soft slab avalanche, of which 90% ran to the ground. The fracture of the two combined slides measured about 1300 feet wide and four to ten feet deep. It ran an amazing 1600 vertical feet. The debris covered nearly a third of the bottom of the path, and filled in a small basin. The depth of the debris was eight to eighteen feet, with the greatest depths amassed at the base of the rock cliffs. A post-incident fracture profile revealed a substantial layer of depth hoar that proved fatal in this instance. The slope angle at the starting zone was from 38 to 40 degrees steep.

> According to Nick Logan with the Colorado Avalanche Information Center, the deposition covered 23 acres. It was 1300 feet long and 800 feet wide.

Lessons Learned:

- The newspaper quoted some of the locals who frequently flirted with the backcountry risks, that skiing out-of-bounds was "better than sex." The question each person who fits this demography should ask himself is, "what will the repercussions be for my friends and family if they have to dig my lifeless body out of a frozen tomb?" Will that also be better than sex?

- Just because a slope has moguls does not make it immune to slides. Peak 7 was covered with moguls on February 18.

- The Peak 7 avalanche drove home the importance of building more comprehensive avalanche education through Colorado Mountain College, the Colorado Avalanche Information Center, the SAR group, and the local ski patrols.

- Search strategy is very important. Take the time to meet with the cooperating dog handlers. Make a plan and stick with it until there is a need for a better strategy.

- Give your dog frequent and regular breaks. Working huge avalanches is exhausting work for the handler and dog. Use the breaks to re-evaluate your strategic plan.

- Whenever possible, introduce the avalanche dogs before initiating search operations. The distraction of a new dog that wants to get acquainted can quickly cause other working dogs to lose their focus.

- Many probe lines were working at the same time. In a few instances, when some probe lines were performing coarse probes, others were doing fine probes. There needs to be more consistency and better communication between probe line leaders.

- Carry marking wands for dog alerts. Make sure that they are a different color than the red, blue, and yellow flags used to mark probed areas, safe routes in and out, and clues. Write, "dog alert" on the flagging. The dog alert wands should remain in place for the entire duration of search operations.

- Always probe before shoveling at a dog alert. Until you have achieved a strike, shoveling is a waste of valuable time and energy.

- Regularly train around fuel-operated machines; i.e., snowcats, snowmobiles, helicopters, and generators.

- Train with distractions. It is unusual to have an opportunity to work a real mission without other rescuers and equipment present on the debris.

Dan probing into a trench to check out an avalanche dog alert, By Bob Winsett

- Do not be afraid to voice any concerns that you have to command when appropriate. If there are measures that can be taken to increase the dogs' effectiveness, then definitely make your requests known.

- Do not always expect avalanche victims to be near the toe of the debris. In this case, all of the victims were located high in the deposition.

- Breckenridge Ski Corporation did an outstanding job caring for the creature comforts of the rescuers. From food and drink to transportation needs, they supplied. They also held regular press conferences to deal with the media's demands and schedules. When command briefs the media regularly, they tend to report more accurately, and do not get in the way of search operations.

Second Creek, Colorado—P. Burnett

Accident: We received a call the evening of January 2, 1988. Friday, New Year's Day, a group of cross-country skiers came upon an old avalanche, nearly covered with new blowing snow, and noticed a ski protruding from it. As they dug down, they were shocked to discover that the ski was attached to a 31 year-old-man's foot. The victim was an experienced backcountry skier, who had been a mountaineering instructor in Wyoming for years.

They reported the accident to the authorities, and learned that the man had been winter camping and cross-country skiing with his 25-year-old friend. Two rescue dog teams were asked to report to the Berthoud Pass Ski Area at 7:00 a.m. the following morning, where they would be picked up and flown in to the site.

Search: It was a bitterly cold morning, minus 20 degrees—typical avalanche search weather. While waiting for our ride, two Labrador Retrievers (not SAR dogs) ran up to Hasty. The larger of the two jumped him and proceeded to chomp on his head. My husband, Dan, pulled the lab off Hasty and wrestled him to the ground. We treated the deep puncture wounds around Hasty's eye in the minutes before our helicopter transport arrived.

Searchers waiting to go into the field, By Dan Burnett

Seventy volunteers from six different rescue units responded to the command post. After ski area patrollers made short order of the hang-fire and freshly loaded snow, we started to work. Hasty had an uncanny ability to focus during SAR missions. This fact was especially apparent during this particular response. Adrenaline still coursing through his veins, Hasty alerted on the woman within two minutes, but in a way that I had not yet encountered. First he

Hasty and Chester leaving the field after Second Creek mission, By Dan Burnett

urinated on the spot and then he started digging. Chester, a Chesapeake Bay Retriever from Eagle County SAR, alerted in the same area. When I diagonally probed the yellow snow, I made a strike. As searchers dug down to the body, both dogs continued searching to verify the absence of other burials. Rescuers dug out the young woman within 15 feet of where her companion's body had been located.

According to the coroner's report, she had been buried six days. I recall feeling strange about finding a woman in an avalanche. Up until this time, I still believed the myth that only men in the twenty-something age bracket were foolish enough to venture into avalanche prone territories. According to Dale Atkins, between 1950 and 1995, nearly half of the avalanche fatalities occurred to people between 20 and 29. Of those, approximately 90% were men. Suddenly, avalanche danger became far more authentic to me. I realized that even I was not immune to white death.

Slide Statistics: This was a hard slab avalanche and the deposition was about 150' by 250'. The slide had occurred around December 29 and was probably triggered by the two cross-country skiers. The avalanche had traveled approximately 650 feet.

Lessons Learned:

- Command should ensure that only rescue dogs are allowed near mission base, as well as the search site.

- Dogs must be trained and socialized in such a manner that they are pre-stressed for the unusual circumstances that search and rescue afford. A dog unaccustomed to the demands of helicopters, frigid temperatures, and unfamiliar dogs will have difficulty focusing on the task at hand.

- You and your dog should be well acquainted with helicopter operations and safety. Understand how to approach the helicopter, as well as the use of seatbelts, helmets, and intercoms. Your dog must have a leash on at all time when in or around a ship and must always behave in a calm and controlled demeanor.

- Always be in control of your dog at base operations. You are your dog's principal advocate, especially in strange, unfamiliar environments.

- Allow the dogs to do a hasty search before initiating your strategic plan. Sometimes they will detect a scent instantaneously and need no further direction. Those are the times you are grateful for all the training you invested in your canines.

- Expect different types of alerts for deceased victims; i.e., rolling, defecating, urinating, low crouching, chicken scratching the snow, whining, etc. Watch for unusual behavior.

- Even after confirming burial locations, continue working the dogs until command has verified that no other victims exist.
- Women are not exempt from the avalanche death statistics.

Sheep Mountain, Montana—B. Gafney

Scenario: On April 3, 2001, two skiers were caught in separate avalanches outside of Bozeman, near Bridger Bowl. The very same day, a 53-year old man from Minnesota was snowmobiling south of West Yellowstone with a party of six. They were familiar with this rugged, hard to access backcountry, and tried to make it an annual event.

Accident: The avalanche path had not yet slid that particular winter; and the man was highmarking when the entire bowl gave way under the pressure of his machine. Having no rescue gear among them, the five other members of the party left the area after a short search.

Search: We got the page about one and a half hours after the accident occurred. Fortunately, I was in town, allowing for a more rapid response. Even more amazing was that Ron Johnson, a member of the SW Montana Avalanche Team, also happened to be there. As fate would have it, Yellowstone National Park had a contract helicopter shuttling researchers out of Bechler. With some smooth negotiating, Ron and I and my SAR dog, Smokey, were able to fly to the accident scene.

I was immediately impressed by the size of the deposition; slabs were the size of automobiles. The upper section had completely released to the ground.

SAR dog Smokey, By Bonnie Gafney

In respect to depth, we could not hit the ground with our probe poles. The buried man's snowmobile had already been located in the lower third of the deposition.

Witnesses reported that the man had been observed, "flying over the handlebars near the top of the slide and then traveling in a different direction than the snowmobile." We completed a thorough search around the uncovered machine, but only found more snowmobile parts.

The terrain caused the avalanche debris to make a 90° elbow, an excellent trap, strewn with huge slabs on the outside corner. Ron and I agreed that this was a good place to concentrate our search efforts. The witnesses' reports confirmed our decision, as the man was last seen "riding up and down in the snow" near the bend.

Smokey worked very effectively, as he focused and ranged in an efficient manner. He had some interest in the middle of the slide path, following a consistent line downhill. Each alert was finely probed. At one of the stronger alerts, shovelers uncovered traces of blood. At first, I thought that Smokey's pads might be bleeding, but such was not the case. The blood obviously came from another source. We spent two hours in the middle of the slide path and the outer elbow, convinced that our victim must be close to the perplexing blood samples. I then decided to change our strategy and move downhill, despite the fact that we had started our efforts from the center of the toe, where the helicopter had dropped us off amid a cloud of helicopter fumes.

Another significant piece of information is that one of the reporting parties had placed a shirt on an outside edge of the deposition, about a third of the distance from the avalanche toe. This was just above and across from where the snowmobile was found. This was also supposedly where one of the members of the snowmobile party had sat on his own machine to observe the slide. We had not searched the area surrounding the shirt in question, on the assumption that a body could not have traveled underneath the observer and his snowmobile. How could it? The snow there could not have been more than a few feet deep. I had even let Smokey check out the shirt itself at one point, and then returned him to his previous assignment.

After a brief strategy break, Smokey resumed his searching with continued enthusiasm. I watched as his head lifted to an airscent and he rushed over to the far flank, about 30 feet below where the shirt had been lying. He scratched around generally; then with no hesitation, he pinpointed an area, and the snow started to fly. I knew that Smokey had him; he was digging with incredible speed and excitement. Before I could even get over to him, my dog had dug such a deep hole that only his tail and butt were visible. Before I knew it, he came out of the hole with a glove that he must have pulled off the victim's hand. I was ecstatic that we had completed our search before dusk, and that Smokey had worked so well.

Unfortunately, the man was dead. He had sustained significant multi-systems trauma. Obvious facial injuries had produced the previously mentioned blood, probably induced when hurtling over the handlebars.

It is my assumption that our earlier alerts were from the travel of the man's body and blood loss through the deposition. I felt a bit sheepish that the search took as long as it did, as I had responded to 12 fatal avalanches, each a little different from the previous one. Five of these accidents were resolved by dog finds. However, snowmobilers are usually found near their sleds or near the toe. In this case, we may have placed more weight on the witnesses' report than we should have. In addition, the obvious terrain traps "trapped us" and deterred us from doing a more thorough search of the entire deposition. Again, live and learn.

Certainly, April 3 was a great day for avalanche dogs. Smokey persevered well; he hot-loaded the helicopter like a professional; and he found his man just the way he had learned. The other rescuers, dreading a multiple day response, were impressed with Smokey's efficiency. Moreover, the friends and family were able to bring closure to their grief.

Slide Statistics: The avalanche was hard slab and it released to the ground. The deposition was more than 12 to 15 feet.

Lessons Learned:

- Snowmobilers must get the same kind of training in avalanche awareness as skiers, snowboarders, and mountaineers. They expose themselves to the same risk, if not greater.

- Before venturing into the backcountry, a person, especially someone from outside the area, should make it their business to consult local avalanche information centers. Perhaps knowledge that Sheep Mountain had not slid yet that winter would have helped the men to make wiser decisions that particular day.

- Rescue beacons and shovels should be standard operating equipment for every snowmobiler.

- Since there were five members of the snowmobile party not buried, two should have gone out for assistance; the remaining three should have continued searching. The best chance of finding an avalanche victim alive is by one of his own party finding him.

- Helicopter crews are our friends. Make every effort to build strong relations with the local helicopter service so that when the need arises, they are prepared to work with you. You and your dog should have a healthy respect and high level of comfort when moving and working around helicopters.

- Strategy breaks are an essential element of avalanche search—essential for the handler and the dog.

- Know the local snow workers so you know who you can trust and call on when you need their help.
- Understand the most likely sites for avalanche victim burials, and formulate your strategy around that information.
- Receive complete witness reports, but take that information with a grain of snow—I mean salt. Things look totally different before and after a slope has slid.
- In most cases where blood has been found in the deposition, the victim's body has been above the blood traces. However, this will not always be the case.
- Expect helicopter, snowmobile, and snowcat fumes to contaminate the snow. Make allowances accordingly.
- Make a thorough search of the deposition, leaving no chunk of debris "unsmelled." Even some of the most benign areas may prove to be potential victim traps.
- Look for buried snowmobilers near their machines.

South Arapahoe Peak, Colorado—P. Burnett

Scenario: With snow falling all weekend, 60 avalanches on the Continental Divide were reported to the Colorado Avalanche Information Center from Friday through Monday. Twenty-two were logged on Saturday alone.

That same Saturday, December 18, 1999, 23-year-old Justin went hiking west of the Eldora Townsite with his Colorado University acquaintance, Martin. Justin was a fifth year senior, working on a double major in communications and humanities, hoping to become a middle school teacher. Clad in heavy jackets, boots, gloves, and goggles, they set out at 9:00 a.m. from the Fourth of July trailhead; their goal was to climb South Arapahoe Peak at 13,397 feet. Friends described both of them as "avid skiers and outdoorsmen, who had considerable backcountry experience." What started out as a beautiful day quickly turned sour, as heavy snow and strong winds moved in. In an effort to get off the mountain rapidly, the friends took a short cut across a snowfield. That decision and the fact that they did not stay together cost a young man his life, just at its prime.

Accident and Slide Statistics: Martin was caught in a south-facing avalanche at an elevation of approximately 11,500 feet. The slide ran on a 36-degree slope, 250 feet wide and about 500 feet long. After being transported about 30 feet, the avalanche came to rest, and Martin was able to extricate himself. He had no idea where Justin was.

Search: Martin had not seen Justin immediately before or during the accident, but searched for his friend until midnight. Twenty-four more rescuers and dogs continued searching the following day, with no success. By Monday, the day Sandy and I searched, efforts were somewhat scaled back because of extreme weather and building hazard.

The debris was only two to five feet deep in the areas we were assigned. Persistently strong winds of 20 to 30 mph and constant snow since Saturday completely filled in the fracture line, rendering it indiscernible. Because of the building avalanche risk in the section above the gully, we were prohibited from entering that area. A searcher thought that he found tracks, believed to be Justin's, leading into the slide. It is interesting that whenever missions become multiple day, people start to grasp for straws. This is an admirable characteristic of SAR personnel. There is an innate desire to hold on to even the slightest ray of hope.

Probe line searching the South Arapahoe Peak avalanche, By Sue Purvis

The following day snow safety measures were employed to mitigate the danger, but unfortunately, the dogs had little interest in the designated search area. It is unusual to search for such an extensive duration and find no clues. With each new day, it became increasingly apparent that Justin might not even be in our targeted avalanche. These thoughts and lack of any strong alerts from the dogs, helped in the decision to suspend mission operations. The hardest part about concluding a search is the agony for the family. Friends and relatives find it nearly impossible to say "goodbye" to a loved one whose body is still missing.

During this ten-day search, nearly ten avalanche dog teams and dozens of rescuers were deployed from various ski patrols and SAR groups. Incident Command was handled by the Rocky Mountain Rescue Group out of Boulder, Colorado.

South Arapahoe Peak, By Rob Savoye

Justin's body was finally located during the spring thaw by a member of Rocky Mountain Rescue Group. He was not even close to the avalanche where the search efforts were concentrated. His family and friends could finally bring closure to a tragic story.

> "He left in the full of life on a positive note."
> —Justin's Mother

Lessons Learned:

- Choose your friends wisely, especially when so much is at stake. Know the extent of their snow safety knowledge and experience. Being an "outdoorsman" does not necessarily qualify a person as a snow safety expert. There is no replacement for actual training in the field with avalanche workers who truly understand snow dynamics.

- Martin and Justin should have stayed together. That decision probably made the difference between life and death.

- The weather in the mountains can deteriorate rapidly. Plan for the unexpected and the worse case scenario. Despite the weather shift, the men should not have taken a short cut through unfamiliar terrain and snow.

- Martin did the right thing in searching for his friend as long as he could. However, it is my belief that slightly larger parties are better than parties of two. With more people, one can go out for help, while the rest continue searching. With more people, there might have been a better chance of searching areas outside of the immediate avalanche.

- Command must always ensure that there is a comprehensive effort to investigate areas surrounding the avalanche itself, especially in cases of unwitnessed slides that include low visibility.

Copper Mountain Ski Patrol Team, Tim Burnham and Eddy, at South Arapahoe Peak, By Jeff Sparhawk

13 Goodbye, My Friend

The Rainbow Bridge

*Just this side of heaven is a place called the Rainbow Bridge.
When an animal dies that has been especially close to someone here, that pet
goes to the Rainbow Bridge.
There are meadows and hills for all of our special friends
so they can run and play together.
There is plenty of food, water, and sunshine,
and our friends are warm and comfortable.
All the animals who have been ill and old are restored to health and vigor;
those who have been hurt or maimed are made whole and strong again, just
as we remember them
in our dreams of days and times gone by.
The animals are happy and content, except for one small thing:
they miss someone very special, someone they left behind.
They all run and play together, but the day comes when
suddenly one stops and looks into the distance.
His bright eyes are intent: his eager body begins to quiver.
Suddenly he breaks from the group,
flying over the green grass, faster and faster.
You have been spotted and when you and your special friend finally meet,
you cling together in joyous reunion,
never to be parted again.
The happy kisses rain upon your face; your hands again caress that beloved
head, and you look once more into those trusting eyes,
so long gone from your life, but never absent from your heart.
Then you cross the Rainbow Bridge together...*
—Author Unknown

Rescue dog handlers go through grieving twice: the first time is when they decide that their partners no longer have the ability to meet the physical demands of missions. With Hasty, I knew that he would continue searching until he took his final breath, but it killed me to watch him drag himself up the morning after any especially arduous mission. That pain continued until the day that he took his final breath. He was a dog who was born to search and when he could not fulfill his purpose, the light went out of his eyes.

It has been three years now since Hasty has been gone, and the wound is still open in our hearts. Every place I go, especially at Copper Mountain, brings back memories of his antics. A surprise to me was the degree of mourning that Sandy, five years old at the time, suffered with Hasty's passing. I do not think that we, as humans, understand the deep bond that develops between two rescue dogs that work and live together.

No dog will ever take Hasty's place. After 107 missions, not to mention "stand-downs," all I can say is "Thank you, Hasty, for being a dedicated SAR worker, wonderful companion, and loyal friend. I always knew that you would do whatever I asked of you with all your heart. The Search and Rescue World was a better place because of you.

Chapter 13 Goodbye, My Friend   197

Hasty taking a chairlift ride with his best friend, By Bob Winsett

A Dogs Prayer
By Beth Norman Harris

Treat me kindly, my beloved Master, for no heart in all the world is more grateful for kindness than the loving heart of me.

Do not break my spirit with a stick, for though I should lick your hand between the blows, your patience and understanding will more quickly teach me the things you would have me do.

Speak to me often, for your voice is the world's sweetest music, as you must know by the fierce wagging of my tail when footsteps fall upon my waiting ears.

When it is cold and wet, please take me inside. For I am now a domesticated animal, no longer used to bitter elements. And, I ask no greater glory than the privilege of sitting at your feet beside the hearth. Though had you no home, I would rather follow you through ice and snow then rest upon the softest pillow in the warmest home in all the land, for you are my god and I am your devoted worshiper.

Keep my pan filled with fresh water, for although I should not reproach you were it dry. I cannot tell you when I suffer thirst. Feed me clean food, that I may stay well, to romp and play and do your bidding. To walk by your side and stand ready, willing, and able to protect you with my life should your life be in danger.

And lastly my beloved master, should the Great Master see fit to deprive me of my health or sight, do not turn me away from you. Rather hold me gently in your arms as skilled hands grant me the merciful boon of eternal rest…and I will leave you knowing with the last breath I draw, my fate was ever safest in your hands.

The Learning Never Ends

Yankee Doodle Basin

Last night, as Sandy and I walked to the car, I anticipated a quiet evening with the family, followed by two well-deserved days off from work. Copper Mountain had hosted a World Cup Ski Challenge the week before and opened a lot of new terrain for our guests. Consequently, I had let many of my family and home responsibilities slip.

Within a minute of loading Sandy in the car, I heard the beginning of my SAR pager tones, tones that I recognize almost as well as the sound of my alarm clock. Following the tones, a dispatcher's voice pleasantly announced, "Attention all avalanche canine units. Rocky Mountain Rescue is requesting an avalanche deployment to an accident near Eldora. Any available units, please call dispatch."

The call was not a surprise, since 186 avalanches had been reported in the State of Colorado over the last six days, primarily in the area surrounding Indian Peaks, Berthoud Pass, Loveland, and Summit County. Still, the first avalanche mission of every season always takes me a little unawares.

My first reaction was to step on the accelerator pedal, immediately launching my GMC Jimmy into a 360-degree spin, which any other time would have been fun since I was in an empty parking lot. However, this time, I was not amused.

I was frustrated that I did not have a cellular telephone or radio to notify dispatch that I was responding immediately. Frustration is often the name of the game in search and rescue. All the way home, I prayed that the victim would be found by the hasty search team—that he would relax enough to preserve what little oxygen surrounded him in the snowpack or air pockets around his face.

I got home to find Beth and Rachel alone, since Dan had driven the block to the Flight for Life Landing Zone. The girls helped me as I threw supplies out of both of my packs, making sure that Sandy and I had the correct equipment, food, water, and clothing to survive the near zero temperatures and plunging wind chills. Children of search and rescue volunteers are the real heroes. The girls fed Sandy, found goggles that had been collecting dust for six months, loaned me glove liners, and fed themselves dinner as Sandy and I rushed out the door.

When I arrived at the LZ, the flight crew informed us that command was probably going to stand the mission down, because of the amount of time that had transpired since the initial slide. As a little background, the reporting party had been telemark skiing with his 29-year-old friend, Joe. They were both experienced backcountry skiers. What had started out as a dismally dry winter suddenly changed gear. The two men had been champing at the bit to ski powder, and the 20" to 50" of new snow that had fallen around Colorado since Thanksgiving, was all the incentive they needed to head out to Yankee Doodle Basin.

Unfortunately they ignored some of the most obvious warning signs of avalanche danger; i.e., widespread collapsing in the snowpack, many naturally released slides, and Colorado Avalanche Information Center ratings of "Considerable Hazard" near and above timberline. CAIC advised backcountry travelers to use extra caution.

The men most likely triggered the large avalanche that caught them some time in the early afternoon. The slide swept the reporting party over a road and into Yankee Doodle Lake. He said that he could feel the snow push him across the lake until the weight of the avalanche finally broke the ice, totally immersing him. As he struggled out of the water, he looked around for his friend to no avail. Totally drenched, he desperately walked for three hours east until he reached the boundary of Eldora Ski Resort, where a snowmaking supervisor drove him to the Lower Patrol Room. Ski patrollers had the reporting party transported to Boulder Community Hospital, to treat severe hypothermia and frost bitten hands and feet.

The ski patrol activated a search mission, in turn notifying Rocky Mountain Rescue and the Sheriff's Office. Rescuers initially responded to the accident site via snowmobiles. When I arrived at the helicopter landing zone, three and one-half hours had already passed. Despite the time issues, command decided we would proceed to the scene.

As I slowly approached the ship, I made a mental calculation of where different clothing and equipment were located in my backpack. Had I remembered my brand new beacon? Could I access my goggles and headlamp once the ship dropped me off in the dark? Did I have the right clothing to stay warm? Had I packed some petroleum jelly to keep Sandy's feet from icing? These were all issues that would not have been as crucial for a typical avalanche response during daylight. I can say for sure that it had been many years since I had responded to a nighttime avalanche mission. Following the last one, I had decided that I did not soon want to respond to another avalanche search after dark.

I hold air medical pilots and nurses in the highest esteem. They are able to maneuver in the dark, in strong swirling winds, under stressful conditions with the greatest of skill and confidence. Rod and Julie exuded optimism that our mission was certainly important and well within the parameters of our abilities. It was a beautiful, clear moonlit night. There was something esoteric about flying over those gorgeous snow covered peaks, knowing full well that one of those peaks had perhaps snuffed out the life of a young man in a silent cloud of death.

With exact GPS coordinates, Rod easily navigated to the accident site, west of Eldora Ski Resort. We could see rescuers' headlamps on the deposition and snowmobile headlights on the road below. Rod decided that our safest LZ was on the road and instructed Julie and I to watch for obstacles. Despite winds that pushed the ship around, Rod landed proficiently, never causing me to doubt his masterful handling of the helicopter controls.

Once on the ground, Julie helped me to unload equipment and my dog, Sandy. They then lifted off to fly in another dog team from Front Range Rescue Dogs. I found myself in the middle of a small group of people, including Tracy, the victim's girlfriend, some Eldora patrollers, and a sheriff's officer. They briefed me on the particulars of the slide, rescue operations, weather conditions, and remaining hang-fire.

They also told me that we would respond with our beacons on receive since there was a beacon search in progress. At first I reluctantly switched my beacon to receive, and then thought differently, remembering other missions where I had gone against my better judgment. By now, four hours had transpired since the accident. To place searchers at risk, in the dark, with very few rescuers on hand to effect a subsequent search was ludicrous. I spoke up and told the team that I would feel better having our beacons on transmit; they agreed.

When we began searching, Sandy rushed around with his typical vigor, excited for an opportunity to work. The slide was about 900 feet wide and had run approximately 600 vertical feet over cliffs and a road, finally dumping into the lake. The elevation was between 11,000 and 12,000 feet. The fracture line was five feet deep and debris chunks ranged from soft to hard slab.

About 30 minutes after our arrival, Flight for Life flew Jeff Sparhawk in with his Labrador Retriever, Kila. Despite frigid temperatures and strong, gusty winds, the dogs worked well. They maneuvered with keen ability on the steep bed surface of the cliffs and made their way skillfully around the large, eerily moonlit, blue colored chunks. They both showed interest in a location above the road. Fine probing was negative. It was possible that the slide had buried one of the men's skis or a pole in *that location. Sandy's strongest alert was in the center of the slide's tow, where the snow entered the icy water. As he ventured out onto the ice, one of his feet would break through every now and then. I was concerned that if he fell into the water, I might not be able to reach him, so I called him off the ice. Jeff called Operations Base to notify them of Sandy's interest in that area. It made sense that the victim might have been swept into the lake since that was where the reporting party had ended up once the slide came to rest.*

Command asked me to do a beacon search of the deposition below the road and I received no signals. I wondered how long a beacon would function submerged in water. I also wondered what distance it would transmit through water. I had not heard of any studies done in that area.

As the clouds began to obscure the moonlight and as the winds increased the hang-fire, radio traffic announced an impending suspension of search operations until the next morning. Before leaving the field, Jeff and I carefully climbed above the cliffs since the dogs had not searched that deposition yet. I was surprised at the consistency of the debris chunks up high. The snow was denser and the chunks were much larger. The winds were twice as strong and I grew increasingly uncomfortable, knowing that we would receive little warning if a subsequent slide were to run.

At the same time, the radio traffic was focusing on a dark shape that rescuers discovered in the middle of the lake on top of the ice and snow. Rescuers, equipped with lights and binoculars, were convinced that the object in question was that of our missing skier. Dispatch paged additional resources to respond to a potential ice and/or water rescue.

As we made our long drive out of the field, we passed various dive and emergency service vehicles, responding to the staging area. Again, I prayed that perhaps this young man would be the beneficiary of a miraculous hypothermia survival.

We walked into the Eldora Lower Patrol Room, to find rescuers and friends of the victim, awaiting news about the mysterious dark object. It was not long before we received reports that the shape was not the missing man, but instead the reporting party's backpack.

We were all extremely disappointed. Had our dogs missed the victim's scent somewhere in the debris? Granted the search conditions were less than ideal with darkness, strong gusts, deep deposition, steep terrain, and frigid temperatures. I dreaded explaining to Tracy that we had not found her best friend, Joe. I also dreaded a sleepless night, wondering what we could have done differently to facilitate a speedy resolution of the mission. I knew that I would have to wake up early to respond to the 6:00 AM scheduled briefing. No more high-speed helicopter deployments for this mission.

The only ray of light in an otherwise discouraging evening came when I walked into the cafeteria. There by the door were my children, Beth and Rachel, and my husband, Dan. Despite attempts to notify them that I would be spending the evening in Boulder, they had made the two-hour trip to drive me home. The Red Cross had set out a tantalizing spread of food. But, I admit that at that point anything edible would have been tantalizing.

Driving home, Dan and I discussed all the "if only scenarios." I knew that there would be fresh dog units arriving the next morning, but I also knew that I could not stay away – wondering where Joe was, why we had not found him. I made a few calls and arranged to meet another dog handler in the morning to carpool over to the accident. However, a little after midnight, our group leader called, telling us that rescuers had found Joe's body.

When the water rescuers got onto the ice, they discovered that the strange dark shape was in fact a backpack. However, since the ice had re-solidified, they had one of the patrollers perform a *beacon search over the top of the lake. He received a signal and discovered Joe's body three feet under the water and ice.*

I, of course, immediately condemned myself, wondering why I had not been able to receive a signal from the edge of the deposition. I had strong suspicions that the victim was in the water, because of Sandy's alerts and the location of the reporting party.

> According to Knox Williams with the Colorado Avalanche Information Center, of the 629 avalanche deaths that have occurred in the United States since 1950, this incident was the fifth that involved drowning.

The next morning, Ed, the Asst. Patrol Director from Eldora, called me to tell me that they had found Joe about 70 feet from the edge of the lake. I had to know how far away Tucker had received the signal from Joe's beacon. I was flooded with relief to discover that he could not pick up the signal until he was standing directly over the body. The 70 feet of water must have blocked the beacon transmission.

My conclusion, after 16 years of experience and many avalanche missions, is that I will never stop learning and wondering at the amazing abilities of our canine partners. As I complete this writing, my dog Sandy, rests at my feet. Those dogs knew where Joe's body had come to rest. They slept well, knowing that they could be proud of their work. I am sure that their dreams also included a prayer that we, as SAR dog handlers, would measure up to their expectations.

"If she would only learn to trust me." Be patient with me buddy. I am sure you share Hasty's and every other SAR dog's dreams.

Glossary

Air-scenting:
A lost person, dead or alive, is continually shedding scent into the air and surrounding terrain features in the form of dead cells. Wind currents pick up the scent and spread it out into cones, sometimes depositing it in different terrain features in the form of scent pools. An airscent dog handler is assigned a sector to search. It is the handler's responsibility to cover that area by strategically working the dog into the wind. Depending on weather, it may be advantageous to work the top of ridges or the bottom of ravines, in order to place the dog's nose where it can contact the victim's scent in the wind or on the ground. The dog works off-lead with its head up, ranging back and forth, as the handler directs, until it reaches the scent of the missing party. The handler must recognize when the dog has found the scent for which it is searching. Airscent is the mode of searching that an avalanche dog employs.

Alert:
A dog indicates to its handler when it has found scent. The most widely recognized alert for an avalanche dog is to dig. Some handlers use brindsels or barking in additional to the dig. More than anyone else, the individual handler should always be more adept at reading his own dog's alerts.

Blocks:
SAR workers use hard chunks of snow to close off the entrance to a training cave, so that loose snow does not slide into the cave during burials.

Brindsel:
A short leather lanyard attached to a search and rescue dog's collar. When the dog has found someone, the dog returns to the handler with the brindsel in his mouth.

CAIC:
Colorado Avalanche Information Center

Command:
In the Incident Command System, Command is whoever is in charge of the incident.

Compression Zone:
This is the area lower in the snowpack where there has been a transition from the steeper slope angles to the run-out zone. Gravitational forces intensify here because this area supports the steeper, heavier, more compacted portion of the slide path. This lower portion of the slope experiences less wind, and consequently there is more air in the snowpack making for a weaker, softer slab. Settlements in the compression zone may initiate a fracture, which can then propagate to stronger, denser, more bonded slabs higher on the path.

Cornice:
A cornice is a snow formation that overhangs the lee side of ridges. With moderate to strong wind, a vortex often causes the snow to deposit on the lee side and the cornices typically form more rapidly with higher humidity.

Cyalume Sticks:
Plastic wands that contain chemical mixtures. When the wand is bent, the chemicals combine to make the stick glow. Cyalume sticks can be affixed to a dog's harness or collar to increase his visibility during night searches.

Deposition/Debris:
Snow that is released from a slope and comes to rest in the run-out area. Avalanche deposition may range in depth from a few inches to 20 or 30 feet.

Depth Hoar:
A snow crystal with generally larger facets that has very little cohesive properties, sometimes known as sugar snow. Dependent upon age and development, depth hoar snow can range from striated, to hollow, to cup shaped crystals. This snow is typically found near the ground, at the bottom of the snowpack.

False Alerts:
Sometimes avalanche dogs alert in the wrong areas. This behavior can be due to a number of factors:

- The frustration of working for a longer time and in larger areas than normal.
- The frustration of searching for subtler scent than normal, which is certainly the case with deep burials and/or deceased victims.
- Encouragement from the handler to dig at a certain place.
- Old scent in the snow.
- Animal scent.
- Surface scent.

The handler must make every effort to discourage digging at false alerts. As a SAR handler becomes more experienced, he will recognize the subtle differences between true and false alerts. Let the dog work and do not be found guilty of encouraging false alerts.

Find:
When an avalanche dog locates a victim, we call it a "find."

FFL—Flight for Life:
Medical helicopter service used for rapid transport of critically injured or ill patients.

Fracture Line Profile:
A hasty or data pit is dug at or near the fracture of an avalanche to analyze the sliding surface, weak layers, height of the crown, elevations, snow temperatures, layer densities, vertical distance, angles, sizes, and classifications.

GPS—Global Positioning System:
An international navigational tool that was first established by the Defense Department. A hand-held GPS receiver intercepts satellite signals. The unit determines the user's position through triangulation methods.

Hang-fire:
This term is used to describe any danger that remains after a slide has occurred. Hang-fire must be mitigated before any rescuers are permitted to enter the avalanche site.

Hasty Pit:
Initially a probe pole is used to identify layers in the snowpack. Then a hole is dug vertically at least a meter wide and 2 meters deep or to the ground,

whichever comes first. Various tests are performed to determine the strength and thickness of the layers, and the shape and size of snow grains.

Hasty Search:
The initial team that is deployed to any type of search or rescue. Their task is to respond rapidly with only life saving equipment and little else.

High Marking:
(Also referred to as high pointing and hammer heading). A method of maneuvering a snowmobile, where the driver makes progressively larger arcs on steep slopes. The innovation of extremely powerful and fast snowmobiles has rendered this practice increasingly popular among winter "motor-heads."

Hot-load:
A method of entering a helicopter while the blades and engines are still engaged. Speed is always a consideration when responding to an avalanche accident. Hot-unloading occurs when the pilot drops a team at an accident site without turning the ship off.

Hot-loading a dog team during an avalanche deployment, By Dan Burnett

Ice Mask:
When an avalanche victim is buried alive and suffocates under the snow, the moisture from his breath caused an ice mask to form around his face.

In-bounds:
The territory inside ski area boundaries.

ICS—Incident Command System:
ICS is the pattern for command, management, and coordination of any emergency response. The system has a proven track record in improving effectiveness and efficiency for multi-agency responses that require common terminology, unified command, and similar protocols. Many rescue organizations, from fire and forest service to SAR, have recognized the value of the ICS.

LZ:
Landing Zone—an area where a helicopter can land safely. Each helicopter service has specific criteria that guide the necessary dimensions, maximum slope angle, potential hazards, etc.

MVP:
Copper Mountain Medical Volunteer Professional. The group is comprised of Nurses, Physicians, and Paramedics who volunteer as an adjunct to the ski patrol. They assist with accidents and perform other ski patrol duties.

OFA:
Orthopedic Foundation for Animals

Out-of-bounds:
The territory outside of the ski area boundaries.

Post-holing:
Walking through uncompacted snow that cannot support a person or dog's weight. When they walk, they sink through the snow up to their knees or thighs.

Ranging:
The SAR dog should be able to work independently from the handler. This means moving away from the handler in a pattern that most optimally using the wind to locate scent. Sometimes the act of ranging will resemble a "Z" pattern depending on slide dimensions and wind patterns.

Reward:
Each dog must have a tangible reward that the handler gives only when the dog has successfully completed the designated objective of a given SAR exercise. It is a good idea to select a reward that fits inside the neck of

a subject's jacket. It must also be something that the dog will kill for—figuratively speaking.

SAR:
Search and Rescue.

SARDOC:
Search and Rescue Dogs of Colorado. SARDOC is an organization of rescue dog handlers and their dogs that are located throughout the state of Colorado. SARDOC sets standards and certification tests to qualify teams for the various disciplines of search dog work; i.e., airscent, trailing, avalanche, water, evidence, etc.

SCRG—Summit County Rescue Group:
A group of Summit County volunteers who perform SAR missions and promote mountain safety awareness. The group functions under the auspices of the Summit County Sheriff's Office.

Skin up:
Skins, placed on the bottom of skis, enable a skier to ski up snowy areas.

Ski Packing:
A method to mitigate early season avalanche hazards. Ski patrollers walk sideways; next to each other tip to tail, down a slope trying to remove air from, and compact, the snowpack.

Slab Avalanche:
Cohesion and the propensity for snow crystals to bond characterize slab avalanches. A slab avalanche is formed when there is a failure within the snowpack, resulting in a block of snow releasing from the remaining snow. Most of the slides that kill people are slab avalanches. Depending on density, slab avalanches can be either hard or soft.

Snow Safety:
Measures taken to mitigate avalanche risk; also called avalanche control.

Starting Zone:
The place on a slope where avalanches typically begin. It is the top of a slide path, where the unstable section of snow breaks loose from the surrounding snow and begins to slide.

Strike:
On avalanche missions, searchers use probe poles to locate buried victims. When a person pokes a victim with a probe pole, they attain a strike.

TG—Temperature Gradient:
The difference in the temperature of the snow within the snowpack. Typically, snow closer to the ground is warmer than snow closer to the air surface. The greater the difference in temperature between the snow near the ground and the snow near the surface, the greater the temperature gradient.

Toe:
The bottom of the avalanche deposition.

Tracking:
This is the method by which some SAR dogs follow a missing person. The dog, often a bloodhound, is trained to follow each step that a person makes. The dog has learned to smell for more than just the scent of the missing party, but also the distinct smell of the disturbed or crushed vegetation and ground.

Trailing:
The trailing dog has a totally different modus operandi. This dog has been trained to find the scent of the missing party wherever it is the strongest, but still with its nose primarily near the ground. When a person walks, the scent is often carried by the wind to locations other than directly under his footprints. There will probably be more scent left on a bush downwind of where a person walked than directly under that person's feet, especially if the person was walking on rocks or pavement.

Wind:
As with a firefighter, the SAR dog handler should constantly be aware of wind directions and speeds. By understanding the nature of the wind at any given time, the handler is able to place the dog in those locations where the dog will be potentially able to receive scent.

SAR dog Hasty, By Bob Winsett

Appendix

Frequently Asked Questions & Answers

Q: *Can I deduct some of my SAR dog expenses?*

A: You may deduct expenses, such as:
- Mileage to and from missions, training sessions, schools, and seminars.
- Equipment such as beacons, skis, boots, shovels, and probes.
- Any veterinarian expenses that directly relate to SAR.
- The registration fees for SAR seminars and obedience classes.
- If your deductions total more than $250, it is necessary to file form 8283. As with all other aspects of SAR dog work, good, detailed documentation will be beneficial.

Q: *Where is your dog's Brandy keg?*

A: Okay, I didn't say they were all good questions. I just tell people that our dogs are working dogs and they do not drink on the job.

Q: *Since my dog is good at finding a tennis ball buried in the snow, would it be a good SAR dog?*

A: Not necessarily. The thing that many people do not understand is that avalanche dog training takes more than a dog with a good nose. A better question is, "Does the handler have what it takes to train a SAR dog?"

Q: Can dogs hear a victim yelling for help from under the snow?

A: Probably, but their tendency is to want to use their noses more than their ears or eyes. I have scratched my head in wonder when I hear of handlers who say their dog found an avalanche victim because the dog heard the victim yelling. How did the handler know that? Typically, subjects who are buried can hear the voices of rescuers on the surface far better than the searchers on the surface hearing the subjects.

Q: What is the hardest aspect of being an avalanche dog handler?

A: I will never get used to finding dead people. Once handlers become so callused that they do not die a little inside every time they look into the face of an avalanche victim, they had better begin looking for another avocation. The second hardest part of being a rescue dog handler is having to bury your canine companion. Ironic, is it not? That our partners who have unburied so many people all of their lives, in the final analysis, have to be buried in the ground, never to be unburied again.

Hasty's last ride, spreading Hasty's ashes over Spaulding Bowl, By Dan Burnett,

Safety Procedures for Avalanche Dog Training

Manpower and Equipment Requirements:

- Subject(s) to be buried. Handlers should make a point of being buried occasionally so they remember to build large enough caves.
- Dog Team—handler and dog.
- Two shovelers for each buried subject.
- Radios for all shovelers, subjects, and dog handlers.
- Beacons for every shoveler and subject, and skill in using them.
- A means of triangulation (wands, skis, poles, bamboo, trees, etc.)
- Insulated pad for subject to lie on.
- Reward for dog (glove, chew toy, squeaky, etc.)

Training Area Considerations:

- Obviously, there should be no avalanche danger in the selected area. Ideally, debris from previous slides is desirable and the most realistic.
- A slope angle greater than 10 degrees helps make shoveling easier.

Snow Cave Construction:

- For greatest safety a previously compacted area is recommended; i.e., avalanche deposition, boot, ski, or machine compaction.
- Avoid having the subject help with the shoveling in order to minimize sweating, which leads to hypothermia and claustrophobia.

- When possible, build the cave a few hours to a day before the scheduled exercise to allow the snow time to set up.

- To increase strength, build the cave with a domed roof and in at least five feet of snow. A shallower snowpack impedes the cave's integrity, especially in Colorado TG snow. The roof of the cave should be a few inches higher than the top of the entryway.

- Caves should have sufficient room for the subject to roll over, as well as to provide adequate air space. The subject should not need to be in contact with the snow, especially above the waist.

- Before having the subject enter the cave, have someone jump on top of the cave with skis to confirm stability.

- Triangulate the cave. Make it obvious to the shoveler, but not to the handler.

Burial Procedures:

- Subject must be dressed warmly with a hat or hood.
- Subject is best positioned on the side.
- Subject has a radio and beacon and knows how to use both. Perform prior testing of both.
- Snow blocks close off the entrance and then loose snow fills the remaining hole.
- Frequent, regular radio checks are made. If at any time the subjects do not answer or ask for removal, the hole is dug out with every means of location (dogs, triangulation, and beacon.)

Shoveler Procedures:

- Shovelers remain in close proximity to the cave.

- Radios are always on, but may be turned down when the handler and dog approach.
- Shovelers try not to allow others to walk or ski over the caves.
- Upon request from the dog handler, shovelers assist in digging the subject out.

General Considerations:

- Upon conclusion of the drill, either collapse the cave or mark it so that it does not become an obstacle for skiers or boarders.
- At no time does completion of the training exercise take precedence over the safety and comfort of the subject.
- Try to keep the subject in the cave between 15 and 30 minutes. Never exceed one hour.

PLEASE NEVER CUT CORNERS OR TAKE CHANCES!

If Caught—Staying Alive

1. Remove as much of your equipment as possible, including skis, poles, backpacks, and snowboards.
2. Use your arms and legs to swim to the surface, trying to move to the side of the avalanche path. Fight for your life.
3. Grab on to trees or rocks if able.
4. If buried, try to move one hand in front of your chest and mouth to create an air pocket, while punching your other hand through the snow to the surface.
5. If possible, try to dig yourself out of the slide.
6. I always find it interesting when I hear people advise avalanche victims to not panic, but it is true. You need to conserve energy.

If Your Friend Is Caught

1. If your friend is going to be found alive, it will be because you are this victim's greatest prospect for staying alive.
2. Develop a safe route out for the eventuality of another avalanche.
3. Determine, and mark, the location where the victim was last seen before disappearing below the surface of the snow.
4. Perform a beacon search if the victim was equipped with a beacon.
5. Probe the area directly downhill from the last seen point (LSP.) Ski poles that convert to probe poles are far more effective than skis. Look for equipment or clothing that may be poking out of the snow. This should not have to be mentioned, but there have been cases where victims could have been found alive had friends been more observant.
6. Go for help only if:
    - There are others who can continue searching,
    - Help is close by, or
    - You are completely exhausted and fear for your own safety.

Avalanche Dog Training Log

Day, Date, and Time: _____

Location: _____

Dog: _____ Handler: _____

Helper/Shoveler: _____ Subject(s): _____

Wind Speed (down, up, crosswind): _____

Temperature: _____ Visibility: _____

Pit Depth: _____ Level of Enthusiasm: _____

Elapsed Time: _____

Problems, Lessons Learned, Future Training Goals:
_____
_____
_____
_____
_____
_____

Search and Rescue Dogs of Colorado SARDOC

Mission Report Form
Individual or SAR dog mission leader fill out within two weeks of mission and return to: SARDOC Coordinator, P.O. Box 1036, Ft. Collins, CO. 80522.

Name of person filing report: _____

Date(s) of mission: _____

Time contacted/completed: _____

Agency that requested dog teams: _____

    Contact person for follow-up: _____

    Phone #: _____

Number/type dog teams requested: _____

Number of SAR dog teams responded to mission: _____

Handler   Dog   Affiliation   Certification   Navigator/Affiliation

_____

_____

_____

Response time of dog team(s) from call out to mission base: _____

Location of Mission (include county and nearest town): _____

Description of victim(s) (age health, sex, etc): _____

Description of scent articles: _____

How victim became lost: _____

Was last seen point well established? _____

How long had victim been missing before dog teams(s) began searching?

_____

Original request came from   1) Own SAR team
                             2) SARDOC Dispatcher
                             3) CSRB
Weather conditions before and during search: _____

Terrain and foliage of search area: _____

Had your assigned area been searched by other teams before your arrival?

_____

Was a dog team responsible for the find? _____

Time spent searching: _____

Briefly, summarize the dog team's role during the search:

PLEASE NOTE: Only avalanche teams that have successfully completed the SARDOC Avalanche Certification may use this form.

Avalanche Deployment Dog Certification Protocols

SUBJECT: AVALANCHE DOG CERTIFICATION
EFFECTIVE DATE: March 1995, Policy Number: 524.75
DATES REVISED: June 1998, January 2000, and January 2001

PURPOSE: To ensure that all Avalanche Dogs participating in Avalanche Deployment meet the standards for certifications, as mandated by Search and Rescue Dogs of Colorado or by Summit County Avalanche Deployment Avalanche Dog Requirements.

POLICY: All Avalanche Dogs participating in Avalanche Deployment will have successfully completed the specialty training and requirements for avalanche certification by SARDOC or Summit County Avalanche Deployment Avalanche Dog Requirements by December 15 of each year. Each year, the Summit County Sheriff or Technician administering the AD program will review the certification of each dog and handler, and an "active" list will be maintained.

1. Avalanche dogs and their handlers will successfully complete training necessary to attain specialty certifications.
2. Avalanche dogs and their handlers will successfully complete helicopter safety annually, by December 15 of each ski season.
3. Avalanche dogs and their handlers will make monthly visits to the helicopter at the Summit Medical Center heli-pad to ensure familiarity with the aircraft.

COMPLIANCE RESPONSIBILITY: FFL Pilots, Nurses, Paramedics, Avalanche Dog Handlers, Sheriff Department
SCOPE: Flight Operations
APPROVAL: _____
  Director/Flight Operations

Used with the permission of the FFL Avalanche Deployment Program.

References & Bibliography

Atkins, Dale. *Avalanche Deaths in the United States*, 1950/51—1994/95.

Bryson, Sandy. *Search Dog Training*. Boxwood Press, Pacific Grove. 1984.

Bulanda, Susan. *Ready to Serve, Ready to Save*. Doral Publishing, Inc., Wilsonville. 1999.

Cairns, Julie. *The Golden Retriever. All that Glitters*. Howell Book House. 1999.

Caras, Roger A. *A Celebration of Dogs*. New York: Times Books, 1982.

Daffern, Tony. *Avalanche Safety: For Skiers & Climbers*. Mountaineers Books, Seattle. 1999

Fredston, Jill and Douglas S. Fesler. *Snow Sense: A Guide to Evaluating Snow Avalanche Hazard*. Alaska Mountain Safety Center, Anchorage. 2001

Fuller, John L. and John Paul Scott. *Genetics and the Social Behavior of the Dog*. University of Chicago Press, Chicago. 1998

Hebard, Caroline and Hank Whittemore. *So That Others May Live, Caroline Hebard and Her Search and Rescue Dogs*. Bantam Books, New York, 1992.

LaChapelle, Edward R. *The ABC of Avalanche Safety*. Mountaineers Books, Seattle. 1985.

Letham, Lawrence. *GPS Made Easy: Using Global Positioning Systems in the Outdoors*. Mountaineers Books, Seattle. 2001.

Masson, Jeffrey Moussaieff. *Dogs Never Lie About Love*. Crown Publishers, NY. 1997.

McClung, David and Peter Schaerer. *The Avalanche Handbook*. Mountaineers Books, Seattle. 1993

Microsoft Encarta Encyclopedia

Monks of New Skete, The. *The Art of Raising a Puppy*. Little, Brown and Company, Boston. 1991.

Pearsall, Milo D. and Verbruggen, M.D., Hugo. *Scent: Training to Track, Search, and Rescue*. Alpine Publications, Inc., Loveland. 1982.

Pryor, Karen. *Don't Shoot the Dog: The New Art of Teaching and Training*. Bantam Doubleday Dell Publishing. 1999.

Randolph, Tom. *Summit County Rescue Group, 25 Years.* C&M Press, Denver, 2000.

Zink, M. Christine, DVM, Ph.D. *Peak Performance: Coaching the Canine Athlete.* Howell Book House, 1992.

Resources

Animal Performance Research Labs—Nutritional & Health Supplements
www.k9power.com

Colorado Avalanche Information Center
www.geosurvey.state.co.us/avalanche

Cyalume sticks
www.complast.com/cyalume

Dog Web site
www.dogwise.com

Electronic lazer sticks™
www.icsinternet.com/sarstore

National Association of Search and Rescue
www.nasar.org

SAR dog products
www.searchgear.com

Search and Rescue Dog List
LISTSERV@APPLE.EASE.LSOFT.COM

Search and Rescue Dogs of Colorado
www.sardoc.org

Specialized Outdoor Goods and Services
www.yuccadune.com

The Avalanche Center
www.csac.org

Westwide Avalanche Network
www.avalanche.org

Index

A
Agility 89
Air-scenting 39
Alert, definition of 63
Article Searches 75
Avalanche
 deployment 119, 121
 dog training log 221
 public relations 137
 rescue beacons 15
 shovel 20
 specialties 10
Avalanche deployment
 certification protocols 224
Avalanche dogs
 better utilization of 133
 proving worth 131
Avalanche rescue beacons
 practicing with 16

B
Bibliography 225
Blind drills 70
Breed selection 36
Breeds
 coat weights 38
 for avalanche 37

C
Cadaver materials 77
Candidacy 7
Certification 103
 preparation 109
 Summit County 109
 testing details 104
Characteristics
 air-scenting 39
 coat weight 38
 off lead 39
 temperament 39
Choosing a dog 84
Collapsible probe poles 18
Collar 17
Commands 51
Commitment, and family life 9
Commitment of time 8
Compass 23
Conditioning 87
Critical Incident Stress 134
Cyalume sticks 22

D
Documentation, and training 52
Dog bowl 21

E
Educational opportunities 138
Electrolyte replacement beverages 92
Equipment 13
 avalanche rescue beacons 15
 avalanche shovel 20
 clothing 19
 collapsible probe poles 18
 cyalume sticks 22
 dog bowl 21
 first aid kit 22
 GPS, compass, maps 23
 leash and collar 17
 radios 21
 skis or snowshoes 19
 strobe light 22
 vaseline 22
 wands 17
 water 21

F
First Aid Kit 22
Frequently Asked Questions 215
Fund Raising 139

G
Glossary 207, 209, 211, 213
GPS 23
Grieving process 196

H
Handler preparation 2
  characteristics 2
  grieving 196
  multiple handlers 56
  ongoing training 5
  types of 4
Head and shoulder cave 65
Health
  and veterinarians 93
  hydration 91
  resting your dog 92
Health factors 80
Hydration 91

L
Leash 17
Lift Evacuation 58
Logistics, search 129
Long Searches 73

M
Maps 23
Media exposure 138
Mission base
  attitudes 130
  logistics 128
Missions 28, 35, 41, 54, 74, 95, 111, 114, 127
  Cottonwood Creek, Colorado 143
  Diamond Peak, Colorado 145
  Factory Hill, Yellowstone 150
  Fourth Steep Gully, Colorado 155
  Francie's Cabin, Colorado 159
  Marvin Gardens, Colorado 163
  Montezuma, Colorado 166
  Mt. Kelso, Colorado 171
  Peak 7, Colorado 173
  Second Creek, Colorado 179
  Sheep Mountain, Montana 183
  South Arapahoe Peak, Colorado 189
  Yankee Doodle Basin, Colorado 199
Mock Searches 76
Motivation 49
Multiple dogs 72
Multiple subjects 71

N
National Avalanche School 5

O
Obedience training 45
OFA 33
Off lead 39

P
Praise and rewards 48
Primary handler 56
Probability of Area (POA) 116
Probability of Detection (POD) 117
Public Relations
  at ski areas 139
  fund raising 139
Puppies 42
  characteristics for SAR 27
  gender 31
  health 87
  selecting 25
  temperament 30
  training 87
Pure-bred dogs 32

R
Radios 21

References 225
Resting between missions 92
Runaway Games 61

S

Safety Procedures 217
SAR Competitions 140-141
SARDOC 4, 222
Scent
   and cold conditions 99
   and snow 98
   and wind 100
   exposure to fumes 118
   length of burial 100
Search strategy 113
   ending a search 122
   risk factors 123
   slow searches 115
   snowmobiles 117
   trust 114
Secondary handlers 56
Sense of smell 97
Shallow, Full Body Cave 66
   with blocks 68
   with blocks and loose snow 69
Shovel, avalanche 20
Skeleton drawing 81
Skis 19
Sniagrab 140
Snowmobiles 117
Snowshoes 19
Socialization 47
St. Bernard 37
Stress Management 134
Strobe Light 22
Structure or form 81
   considerations 83

T

Temperament 30, 39
The Rainbow Bridge 195

Training 5, 43
   agility 89
   article searches 75
   blind drills 70
   body language 53
   cadaver materials 77
   commands 51
   conditioning 87
   deeper cave 70
   documentation of 52
   for cold conditions 99
   for scent 97
   head and shoulder cave 65
   hydration 91
   lift evacuation 58
   long searches 73
   methods to avoid 46
   mock searches 76
   multiple dogs 72
   multiple subjects 71
   obedience 45
   praise and rewards 48
   progression 61
   runaway games 61
   socialization 47
   when to start 45

V

Vaseline 22
Veterinarians 93
Volhard Puppy Aptitude Test 30
Volunteering 6

W

Wands 17
Warm Clothing 19
Water 21
Weight 89
Wilderness airscent 10
Wind 100
Winter Coats 38